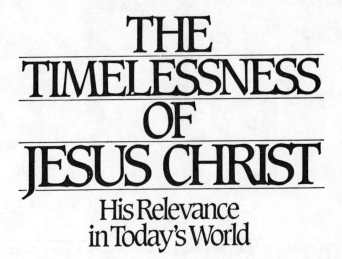

THE TIMELESSNESS OF JESUS CHRIST

His Relevance in Today's World

RICHARD C. HALVERSON

Regal Books

A Division of GL Publications
Ventura, CA U.S.A.

The foreign language publishing of all Regal books is under the direction of Gospel Literature International (GLINT). GLINT provides financial and technical help for the adaptation, translation and publishing of books for millions of people worldwide. For information regarding translation, contact: GLINT, P.O. Box 6688, Ventura, California 93006.

Scripture quotations in this publication are primarily the author's own paraphrase. Also quoted is the Authorized King James version.

Published by Regal Books
A Division of GL Publications
Ventura, California 93006
Printed in U.S.A.

Library of Congress Cataloging in Publication Data

Halverson, Richard C.
    The timelessness of Jesus Christ.

    1. Jesus Christ—Person and offices.
2. Christianity—20th century.   3. Church and
the world.   4. Moral conditions.   I. Title.
BT202.H256   261.1   82-80008
ISBN 0-8307-0838-3   AACR2

To the officers and congregation of Fourth
Presbyterian Church whose friendship,
encouragement, fatherly and brotherly guidance
have been one of life's richest benefits through
more than twenty-two years of ministry.

"Ironically, those whose slogan is relevance may be the ones who most risk being swept along passively and blindly by the march of time. It sometimes seems as though they would preserve Christianity in the world by baptizing as 'Christian' whatever they find thriving in the world: psychotherapy . . . urban renewal . . . sexual revolution . . . and finally, atheism. . . .

"There is grave risk that the seeming 'relevance' of special ventures, such as direct social action, may be an evasion of the responsibility to respond to God in one's own station and to set right the affairs of one's own life."

From the *Princeton Seminary Bulletin*, June, 1967, by James E. Dittes, Faculty of Yale Divinity School, entitled, "The Relevance of Being Irrelevant."

Contents

Then said Jesus, Father, forgive them; for they know not what they do. And they parted his raiment, and cast lots.

And the people stood beholding. And the rulers also with them derided him, saying, He saved others; let him save himself, if he be Christ, the chosen of God.

And the soldiers also mocked him, coming to him, and offering him vinegar, and saying, If thou be the king of the Jews, save thyself.

And a superscription also was written over him in letters of Greek, and Latin, and Hebrew, THIS IS THE KING OF THE JEWS.

And one of the malefactors which were hanged railed on him, saying, If thou be Christ, save thyself and us.

Luke 23:34-39

Chapter 1

The Illusion of Relevance

Emerging out of the political campaign of 1980 is a significant and potentially disastrous phenomenon: the almost total preoccupation of conservative evangelicals in the political processes. Though not an unmixed blessing, in the very nature of incarnational faith, Christians *ought* to be involved in translating faith into life in this world; the danger is that secondary issues are given priority to the neglect of essentials. In the sixties it was the liberals who were going to change the world by political processes. Will evangelicals abandon their unique solution for human changes—the gospel—for political means?

It is incumbent on those who pray weekly, "Thy will be done in earth as it is in heaven," to do all in their power to seek for kingdom-of-heaven conditions in their situations and to act as though they mean what they ask in their prayers; however, it is clear in Scripture that the will of God is preeminently for the *eternal* welfare of mankind, not simply his earthly condition here and now.

Anger over an ever-increasing bureaucracy with its exorbitant taxes, its growing centralized control, its mounting deficit, its dehumanizing legislation, its immorality, its indifference to spiritual and eternal realities is understandable; but such emotion ought not to replace an evangelical compassion, concerned for the eternal lostness of mankind.

Jesus Christ remains as always the central issue in history. It is fundamental to biblical faith that no human system is ordained to pass over into eternity as the kingdom over which Christ reigns. Every other issue in history is secondary to the eternal issue of man's salvation. It would be tragedy in the first magnitude if those who alone profess to be committed to the eternal salvation of mankind somehow were diverted to issues which are transitory and earthly.

One thing is sure: if Bible-believing Christians, so-called, neglect the primary purpose of Christ's entrance into history, there are no others who will take up the cause! Evangelicals have been guilty of neglecting social responsibility in the past in their commitment to the gospel; but there is certainly no justification for neglecting the gospel in their zeal for social issues which have their ultimate resolution in the proper application of the gospel. The life and ministry of Jesus established the model.

According to the record, Jesus gave sight to three blind men, made the deaf to hear, the dumb to speak, the crippled to walk. He cleansed lepers and, in three instances, raised the dead. On two occasions He fed huge crowds with a few scraps of food. In short He did a great deal to alleviate human suffering and wretchedness in His three short years of ministry. He attacked frontally the universal enemies of humanity: disease, poverty, famine and death. Did He do this for all who were smitten? That is, did He heal all who were diseased, give speech to all who were dumb, hearing to all who were deaf, cleansing to all who were lepers, wholeness to all who were crippled? Did He feed all who were hungry? Did He raise all who were dead? The answer, of course, is He did not! Well if not, why not? If He could do this for some, why not more? Why not all? If He could touch blind eyes and make them see, why would He leave anybody blind? If He could take a few loaves and fishes and feed fifteen to twenty thousand people, why should anybody go hungry? Was He unaware that there were others who were blind and deaf and dumb and leprous and hungry? Hardly. If He was aware of this need all about Him was He indifferent to it? One cannot believe this about the man who is preeminently the prototype of human compassion and love. Had He reached the limit of His ability to do these things? Had He run out of power? This is hardly reasonable.

For that matter why did He let Himself be crucified? He said He was in control of this. He said very clearly, "No man takes My life from Me, I lay it down of Myself; I take it up again. I have the power to lay it down, I have the power to take it up again" (John 10:18). When He stood before Pilate, Pilate was aggravated by His silence and under the pressure of that decisive moment said to Him: "Speak to me, don't you know I have the power to crucify you or the power to release you?" Jesus responded by saying, "You have no power over Me at all, except it be given you from above" (John 19:10,11). Many times His enemies tried to take Him in the course of His three-year ministry, always without success. Finally, when He was apprehended in the garden, He Himself approached those who came after Him with swords and staves, offering Himself to them. He said to His disciples, "My time is at hand." His final word on the cross was "Finished! Father, into thy hands I commend my spirit," as though what He had come to do was accomplished. Then the record says, "He gave up the ghost." He died on the cross, voluntarily. He literally laid down His life by sheer volition.

If Jesus Christ had such remarkable, final control of His destiny, why did He not refuse crucifixion, remain alive, and devote Himself to the elimination of all human wretchedness and tragedy? Why did He submit to crucifixion? This question, you see, is really implicit in the mockery that taunted Him on the cross. Three times, it is recorded in Luke 23, He was challenged—the rulers: "If He be

Christ let Him save Himself" (v. 35); the soldiers: "If you are the King of the Jews, save yourself" (v. 37); and even the thief: "If you are Christ save yourself and us" (v. 39)!

Implicit in their challenge is the matter of relevance—the relevance of Christ to history, to human need. Definition is fundamental to the understanding of our responsibility as Christians in this contemporary world which is demanding relevance. What is relevance? Is it a pragmatic test, meaning, does a thing work? Even more personally, does it work for me? Does it work in my situation? Does it address itself to the real problem? Does it give answers that are valid? Will it work? The word *relevance* cannot stand in isolation because it involves relationship. It means to be related, to be appropriate, to be germane, to be suitable. It can be understood only in application to objects or things or people or circumstances. In other words, when one asks, "Is Christian faith relevant?" it is quite proper to reply, "Relevant to what?"

The challenge of relevance, explicit or implied, can be very subtle, seductive and intimidating to evangelicals. It is precisely in this context that Christian faith is being tested today, and not uncommonly—on the basis of inverted values—repudiated. In the name of relevance there is insistence that Christianity serve one human system or another; and if it does not work for whatever system championed it is presumed irrelevant or invalid, null and void.

Some say Christianity must be socialistic or capitalistic, liberal (economically, politically and sociologically, that is), or conservative. Christianity must serve segregation or integration, democracy or totalitarianism. By such false criteria Christians are being divided. There are Republicans who honestly believe a Democrat cannot be a Christian, and Democrats who feel the same way about Republicans. There are those who say a Christian cannot be politically liberal; others who insist a Christian cannot be politically conservative. People are locking the gospel of Jesus Christ to human systems and demanding relevance on their limited terms. If Christianity does not produce on their terms it is rejected, just as Jesus Christ was rejected as He hung on the cross, and for the same general reason.

The issue is clearly drawn in the challenge of the thief, "If thou be Christ save thyself and us." Such was the contempt of this criminal for the dying Saviour! And Jesus has been indicted with such a challenge in every generation to the present moment, even by many of His friends, so-called. Now the thief had a false idea of *Christ's purpose*—"If thou be Christ save us." As far as he was concerned the integrity of Jesus Christ rested on his own personal, immediate physical relief. "Get me out of this mess or you are not Jesus Christ." He was saying, in effect, prove you are Messiah by getting me off this cross and out from under the penalty of my life of crime. He was laying down the conditions under which he would take Jesus Christ seriously. He was saying, "You conform to my demands, and I will believe you." The world has been requiring this or its equivalent ever since.

The number is legion today of those who put the conditions under which they will honor God! As far as they are concerned, like the thief, Christ is to be judged according to their own personal interpretation, their own criteria for relevance; and if Christ is to be acceptable He must conform to their standards.

One fact is uniform in these

demands—the criteria for relevance is always worldly in the sense of "this world-liness," life this side of the grave, physical life. In whatever pious context it is put, Christ is judged on commercial grounds which involve primarily self-interest. (Not always, of course; for Christ is often judged on so-called humanitarian grounds.) For example, people have angrily left churches because they would rather nurse their prejudices about blacks than be Christian about it.

Some put it this way: the Christian hope is "pie in the sky by-and-by." This half-truth, which incidentally betrays abysmal ignorance of Christian eschatol-ogy, this cliché, implicit in which is the idea of relevance, has been used to ridi-cule Christian faith for more than half a century. And the incredible fact is there are those today in the church, even clergy, who still fall for this ludicrous bait and write the gospel off as irrelevant. They are like the thief on the cross. "If you are Christ save us!" They fail completely to understand Christ's purpose in history.

The thief also had a false idea of *the Messiah*. He was not only completely wrong as to the purpose for which the Messiah entered history; he was completely wrong as to the means whereby this purpose was to be achieved. He said, "If thou be Christ save thyself." One never ceases to be amazed at the stubborn and perennial conspiracy to eliminate the crucifixion from Christian faith. It must be masterminded by some transcendent force. Even Peter tried.

Minutes after Peter made his great confession, Jesus began to prepare His disciples for His "rendezvous" in Jerusalem where He would "suffer many things from the chief priests and the elders and the scribes, and be crucified and rise again" (Matt. 16:21). The record reveals that "Peter took Him and rebuked Him, and said in effect, 'No, Lord, you are not going to do this' " (v. 22).

The two disciples on the road to Emmaus, following the crucifixion, were convinced that Jesus' death was a terrible, tragic mistake, the end of their hopes and the complete frustration of His historical purpose (see Luke 24:21).

So did the Jewish leaders in this text, "The rulers derided Him, saying, 'He saved others; let Him save Himself, if He be Christ, the chosen of God.' " You prove you are the Messiah by coming down off that cross.

"The soldiers mocked Him, coming to Him and offering Him vinegar and saying, 'If thou be the King of the Jews, save thyself' " (23:36,37). This recurring effort on the part of humanity—within the church as well as without—to remove the cross of Christ from Christian faith, is monotonous by its regularity and its consistency.

Jesus Christ's purpose in history transcends all the ideas and systems and utopias of men. It is an eternal purpose only in terms of which history has meaning; and this purpose required that He lay down His life on the cross. The crucifixion of Jesus Christ is God's ultimate remedy. As the cure is to the disease, so the cross is to human need. Anything less is temporary, as relief is to symptoms.

Take one social evil, for example, crime, in one limited area, metropolitan Washington. Suppose it were decided to eliminate crime in Washington, D.C. Suppose it were possible to prevent crime from being imported into the city so that you were dealing with the problem as it now exists. What legislation, what organization, what education would it take? And how much would it cost? Is it possible to eliminate crime by any social program, by any human effort? How about poverty? Drug abuse? Alcoholism? Racism?

How about war? At the Japanese surrender ceremony following the Pacific war, General Douglas MacArthur said: "Military alliance, balances of power, League of Nations all in turn have failed, leaving the only path to be by way of the crucible of war. The utter destructiveness of war now blots out this alternative. We have had our last chance. If we do not devise some greater and more equitable system, Armageddon will be at our door. The problem basically is theological and involves a spiritual recrudescence and improvement of human character that will synchronize with our almost matchless advance in science, art, literature and all material and cultural developments of the past two thousand years. It must be of the spirit if we are to save the flesh."

In an editorial in *U.S. News and World Report* of May 5, 1956, the late David Lawrence wrote, "It is a temporary answer to the threat of world disturbance that we face. The North Atlantic Treaty is temporary. The United Nations is temporary. All our alliances are temporary. Basically, there is only one permanence we can all accept. It is the permanence of a God-governed world. For the power of God alone is permanent. Obedience to His laws is the only road to lasting solutions of man's problems."

Consider a statement made by Mario Savio, the twenty-two-year-old philosophy major at the University of California, Berkeley, who was the leading figure in the free-speech movement which exploded in the sixties. Savio was addressing the Trotskyites Young Socialist Alliance, explaining the student protest to them. He said: "The most important concept for understanding the student movement is Marx's notion of alienation. Its basic meaning is that the worker is alienated from his product, but the concept is applicable to students too. Students are frustrated. They can find no place in society where alienation doesn't exist, where they can do meaningful work. Despair sets in, a volatile political agent. The students revolt against the apparatus of the University. This is the motive power of the student movement!"

Amazing, a brilliant, articulate, militant student leader diagnoses the root problem as alienation and meaninglessness or purposelessness. It is almost as if he is drawing from Scripture. Why did

Jesus Christ enter history and lay down His life on the cross? Because men were alienated from God, therefore from each other, and life had no meaning; they were lost! Jesus' purpose was to reconcile men to God so they would no longer be aliens from God and each other. Is it not interesting that the heart of Christian faith addresses itself precisely to the problem that this student leader speaks about at the University of California? This is relevance.

Now back to the question. Why did Jesus Christ not remain alive and eliminate, generation by generation, all the evils which beset humanity? Because He is the Great Physician, and in the finest tradition of medical science He is unwilling to be preoccupied with the symptoms when He can destroy the disease. Jesus Christ, the Great Physician, is unwilling to settle for anything less than elimination of the cause for all evil in history.

The picture is ludicrous but it is analogous. Suppose years ago medical science had decided it was wasting its time and money and energy on this business of research into the disease of poliomyelitis, for example, "Take all the money spent on research and build iron lungs. When people get polio an iron lung will be available, free." Can you conceive, somewhere in the future, a civilization sustained by iron lungs!? Millions of people, having contracted this disease, kept alive by iron lungs.

This is precisely what our modern world is asking Christianity to do in principle. Thank God, the Son of God was the Great Physician. He knew that poverty, prejudice, human wretchedness, tragedy, war and death were due to a malignancy in the human heart which required His own sacrifice on the cross. He came into history and went to Jerusalem and the cross to solve this problem once for all and forever. "I am not ashamed of the gospel of Christ for it is the power of God unto salvation to everyone that believes, to the Jew first, and also to the Greek" (Rom. 1:16). That is relevance! "The blood of Jesus Christ, God's Son, cleanses from all sin" (1 John 1:7). That is relevance.

How is the gospel relevant?

How is love relevant to loneliness?

Hope to despair?

Direction to drift?

Purpose to meaninglessness?

Fulfillment to frustration?

How is food relevant to hunger?

Water to thirst?
Light to darkness?
Rest to exhaustion?
Life to death?
Resurrection to the grave?

Because that, when they knew God, they glorified him not as God, neither were thankful; but became vain in their imaginations, and their foolish heart was darkened.

Professing themselves to be wise, they became fools, and changed the glory of the uncorruptible God into an image made like to corruptible man, and to birds, and fourfooted beasts, and creeping things.

Wherefore God also gave them up to uncleanness, through the lusts of their own hearts, to dishonour their own bodies between themselves: who changed the truth of God into a lie, and worshipped and served the creature more than the Creator, who is blessed for ever. Amen.

For this cause God gave them up unto vile affections: for even their women did change the natural use into that which is against nature: and likewise also the men, leaving the natural use of the woman, burned in their lust one toward another; men with men working that which is unseemly, and receiving in themselves that recompense of their error which was meet.

And even as they did not like to retain God in their knowledge, God gave them over to a reprobate mind, to do those things which are not convenient; being filled with all unrighteousness, fornication, wickedness, covetousness, maliciousness; full of envy, murder, debate, deceit, malignity; whisperers, backbiters, haters of God, despiteful, proud, boasters, inventors of evil things, disobedient to parents, without understanding, convenant-breakers, without natural affection, implacable, unmerciful: who knowing the judgment of God, that they which commit such things are worthy of death, not only do the same, but have pleasure in them that do them.

Romans 1:21-32

Chapter 2

Righteousness Exalts a Nation

"Righteousness exalts a nation, but sin is a reproach to any people." The timeless truth of that proverb (14:34) is the verdict of the record of every civilization, empire and nation in history. Its relevance for our times is indisputable. In a day when spiritual and moral structures are disintegrating, when the social order is threatened by a narcissism bordering on anarchy, when pervasive skepticism and mistrust are eroding human relationships, no word of truth deserves our attention more than this.

This text is not a threat; it is not even a

warning. It is simply a statement of fact. It is like saying, "The shortest distance between two points is a straight line." It is like saying, "Water equals two parts hydrogen, one part oxygen." It is like saying, "Fire burns, cold freezes." This test is a simple statement of principle, a law of life which is inherent in the universe, in the world, in human nature, in history.

"Righteousness exalteth a nation but sin is a reproach to any people." These remarkable words assert the simple fact that spiritual and moral health is constructive and beneficial, that spiritual and moral sickness is destructive. This is without controversy. The decline and fall of every great social, political, economic order and/or system in history is profound confirmation of the truth of this text. This basic principle is working every day in the life of every person in the world. It is operative every day in home and family life, in all the structures of our nation, in all of the departments of life. Its process is inexorable despite every effort of sophisticated man to rationalize and disregard it. The fruit of righteous living blesses any nation. The degeneration, disintegration and demise of any and all people are inevitable if righteousness is abandoned.

There is simply no argument against this.
This is a simple fact of life, whether we
accept it or not; whether we like it or not.
This is the way things are.

Paul, an observer of the rapid decline
of Rome from its greatness to its corrup-
tion in Nero's day, provided a classic commentary on the negative aspect of Proverbs 14:34—"sin is a reproach to any
people"—in his Epistle to the Romans.
One commentator says of Paul's day:

> When Paul and the other apostles
> were called to enter upon their
> important duties, the world was
> in a deplorable and yet most
> interesting state. Both Heathen-
> ism and Judaism were in the last
> stages of decay. The polytheism of
> the Greeks and Romans had been
> carried to such an extent as to
> shock the common sense of man-
> kind, and to lead the more intelli-
> gent among them openly to reject
> and ridicule it. This skepticism
> had already extended itself to the
> mass of the people, and become
> almost universal. As the transi-
> tion from infidelity to supersti-
> tion is certain, and generally

immediate, all classes of the people were disposed to confide in dreams, enchantments, and other miserable substitutes for religion.

The two reigning systems of philosophy, the Stoic and Platonic, were alike insufficient to satisfy the agitated minds of men. The former sternly repressed the best natural feelings of the soul, inculcating nothing but a blind resignation to the unalterable course of things, and promising nothing beyond an unconscious existence hereafter. The latter regarded all religions as but different forms of expressing the same general truths, and represented the whole mythological system as an allegory, as incomprehensive to the common people as the pages of a book to those who cannot read. This system promised more than it could accomplish. It excited feelings which it would not satisfy, and thus contributed to produce that general ferment which existed at this period.

Among the Jews, generally, the state of things was hardly much better. They had, indeed, the form of true religion, but were in a great measure destitute of its spirit. The Pharisees were contented with the form; the Sadducees were skeptics; the Essenes were enthusiasts and mystics.

Such being the state of the world, men were led to feel the need of some surer guide than either reason or tradition, and some better foundation of confidence than either heathen philosophies or Jewish sects could afford. Hence, when the glorious gospel was revealed, thousands of hearts, in all parts of the world, were prepared by the Grace of God to exclaim, 'This is all our desire and all our salvation!'[1]

The inevitable destructiveness of sin was never analyzed more accurately than Paul's description in Romans. He records the vicious, downward spiral, the awful abyss into which humanity inescapably sinks through sin. A description of the descent begins in chapter 1, at the twenty-first verse: "Because when they knew God they did not glorify Him as God nor were they thankful. . . ." This is the root of sin—failure or refusal to worship God. This is secularism, the spirit opposed to faith in God. Paul could have written, "Godliness exalteth a nation, secularism is a reproach to any people."

The diagnosis continues, "When they knew God they did not glorify Him as God" nor were they "thankful" to Him as God. With what result? They "became vain in their imaginations and their foolish hearts were darkened. Professing themselves to be wise they became fools." Intellectual and emotional degeneration are inevitable when men refuse God, when they are thankless.

Next comes spiritual degeneration (v. 23). These wise fools whose intellect was darkened because they would not acknowledge God, "changed the glory of the incorruptible God into an image made like corruptible man, to birds, four-footed beasts and creeping things." At which point God lets go and social degeneration follows (v. 24): "Wherefore God also gave them up."

Here is a significant fact. Every parent sooner or later must come to this decision with a child who is insubordinate. He may scold and punish and deprive, but if the child insists on rejecting discipline, the time comes when the parent must give him up to his own destructive way. He just has to let him go. "God gave them up." A whole humanity God gave up "to uncleanness through the lusts of their own hearts, to dishonour their own bodies between themselves."

The ineluctable process continues (v. 25): They "changed the truth of God into a lie." (Here is a 180-degree spiritual and moral inversion: black is white, error is truth, chaos is order.) They "changed the truth of God into a lie and worshiped and served the creature more than the Creator."

Now comes the terrible consequences, the perversion of personality (vv. 26,27): "For this cause God gave them up unto vile affections: for even their women did change the natural use into that which is against nature: likewise also the men, leaving the natural use of the woman, burned in their lust one toward another; men with men working that which is unseemly, and receiving in themselves [that is, receiving in their own personalities] that recompense of their error which was meet."

Finally, beginning at verse 28, complete degeneration: "Even as they did not like to retain God in their knowledge . . ." (note the recurring cause is intellectual abandonment of God), "Even as they did not like to retain God in their knowledge, God gave them over to a reprobate mind." There is no power on earth to stop the human mind from becoming reprobate if we reject God. The mind that will not worship God becomes corrupted. This is as inescapable as fire's burning. "God gave them over to a reprobate mind to do those things which are not convenient."

Now you see total breakdown: "Being filled with all unrighteousness, fornication, wickedness, covetousness, maliciousness; full of envy, murder, debate, deceit, malignity; whisperers, backbiters, haters of God, despiteful, proud, boasters, inventors of evil things, disobedient to parents, without understanding, covenant-breakers [contract breakers] without natural affection, implacable, unmerciful." Then in verse 32, the very ultimate in human degradation: "Who knowing the judgment of God, that they which commit such things are worthy of death, not only do the same, but have pleasure in them that do them." They want to see it on the screen, on the stage; they want to read it in books; they want it in advertising. It is not enough to do it; they want to see it done; they take pleasure in it; they are entertained by it. There is nowhere else to go! This is the dead end. This buildup of degeneration in human personality, collectively and individually, winds up (or down) to the ultimate in depravity—vicarious enjoyment of lust, depravity, sin. Sin is entertainment!

But this is ancient literature, written nineteen hundred years ago! What of our contemporary world? *Time* magazine, March 5, 1965, reported that progressive church thinkers now state that "the twentieth century sexual revolution directly challenges Christianity's teachings, biblical teaching against fornication and adultery. As an alternative they propose an ethic based on love rather than law, in which the ultimate criterion for right and wrong is not Divine command but the individual's subjective perception of what is good for himself and his neighbor in each given situation." In other words, I am my own law! I decide what is right for me. You decide what is right for you. *Time* continues: "Church leaders are quoted as saying that no sexual relationship should be absolutely condemned by the church."

Then Joseph Fletcher of the Episcopal Theological School is quoted as saying: "One enters into every decision-making moment armed with the wisdom of the culture" (the wisdom of a Godless, therefore reprobate, mind), "but prepared in one's freedom to suspend and violate any rule, except one must as responsibly as possible seek the good of one's neighbor."

The truth about atheistic existentialism is manifest. The evil in this popular philosophy is being exposed now that the fruit of its teaching is beginning to mature. What is difficult to comprehend is the fact that some intellectuals accept its teachings and conclusions as modern! They are as ancient as Nero's Rome, indeed more ancient. Isaiah wrote seven hundred years before Christ, twenty-six hundred years ago, "All we like sheep have gone astray; we have turned every one to his own way" (53:6). Isaiah did not call it "situational ethics," he called it *sin* (iniquity). Consider Proverbs 12:15, "The way of a fool is right in his own eyes," or Proverbs 21:2, "Every way of a man is right in his own eyes." The labels may be new, but the idea is an ancient one! Call it what you will, it is spiritual and moral anarchy. The twentieth century is no more immune to its decay than the first or the eighth B.C.

Without abrogating the principle of human rights or the efficacy of the present movements, nevertheless it is significant that even these important "rights" movements have been infected by anarchy and narcissism. One leader defined civil rights as a "blank check payable on demand." Why is not more said about civic responsibility? Rights without responsibility do not beget freedom but lead ultimately to chaos and bondage. However evil has been the exploitation of the past; irresponsibility is not a solution. Two wrongs do not add up to a right.

Twelve years ago it was reported by *Christianity Today* that a group of protestant clergymen had formed a Council on Religion and Homosexuals, purportedly to establish dialogue between homosexuals and the religious community. A spokesman declared that one of their purposes was to get a law passed which does not discriminate against homosexuals! The article went on to say that the group's first big showdown came at a fund-raising ball

for the benefit of homosexuals which the
ministers helped to sponsor. Police broke
up the ball and arrested five men and a
woman; two of the men were charged with
lewd conduct on the dance floor after
being officially warned against public intimacies. And then the quote adds that the
ministers protested the police intrusion!

Another news item in the magazine
reported that the Judson Memorial Bap-
tist Church in New York's Greenwich Vil-
lage had a dance program which included
a number in which a man and woman,
both naked, moved across the stage in
face to face embrace! "Knowing the judgment of God, that they which commit
such things are worthy of death, not only
do the same, but have pleasure in them
that do them." There is no mystery about
the popularity of modern pornography
and obscenity. Pleasure in such things is
consistent with a Godless existentialism.

An autobiography written some years
ago, *My Life and Loves* by Frank Harris,
contains the author's account of the four
hundred times he seduced women, giving
in clear, candid, careful detail his tech-
nique from the beginning of the seduction
to its consummation. That book and
many more like it written by former wives

and lovers is available on bookstands competing with popular magazines and movies explicit in their portrayal of the intimacies of sex. This is the ultimate in depravity—pandering pornography to a culture which eats it up.

The point Paul makes in Romans 1 is plain and indisputable: sin leads to individual and collective ruin. Sin guarantees the breakdown of all human social systems; and there is only one solution to this breakdown, "Righteousness exalts a nation" (Prov. 14:34).

The word *righteousness* in both Hebrew and Greek is a simple word. In this day when much dialogue is nothing more than semantic duel, people are rationalizing the meaning of words. This is part of the perversion that is inherent in a Godless culture. But the word is clear in Hebrew and in Greek. It means rightness, justice, virtue. It means to be chaste. It is implied in some of these good old-fashioned words that even Madison Avenue must use today when it wants to appeal to something more than emotion—words like quality, integrity, honesty, responsibility. It means to be right with God and right with your neighbor. It means purity in motive as well as propriety in method. It means reverence for God and concern for others. It means square-play, truthfulness, unselfishness, humility, kindness, charity. It means Christ-likeness.

Unquestionably, we have been looking at a rather dismal scene, but, thank God, there can be another chapter. And that chapter can be written by you and me— that is, if we are willing to pay the price for authentic relevance. But if we go about our daily affairs absolving ourselves of responsibility we actually become a part of the problem that is ravaging our nation and our world. The solution begins with us as persons. Each of us in his own way can become an instrument in the hands of God for reconciliation. If we have the determination to be Christ-managed, we will become an influence for righteousness right where we are. If we have the courage to speak when we are intimidated to silence, and if we are willing to be silent when we ought not to speak, God will lead us by His grace, through His Spirit.

The disciple is not above his master, nor the servant above his lord. It is enough for the disciple that he be as his master, and the servant as his lord. If they have called the master of the house Beelzebub, how much more shall they call them of his household?

Fear them not therefore: for there is nothing covered, that shall not be revealed; and hid, that shall not be known. What I tell you in darkness, that speak ye in light: and what ye hear in the ear, that preach ye upon the housetops. And fear not them which kill the body, but are not able to kill the soul: but rather fear him which is able to destroy both soul and body in hell.

Matthew 10:24-28

Chapter 3

Reasonable Fear

There are fears which are irrational, unnecessary, illusory, unfounded. Jesus often counseled against fears, "Fear not, little flock . . ." (Luke 12:32); "Let not your heart be troubled" (John 14:1). But there is a fear that is rational, real and redemptive. Jesus also commanded "Fear." Fear is a valid motive. We teach a child to fear fire. We instruct a little girl to fear the man who attempts to pick her up in his car when she is walking home from school. The wise parent and counselor makes sure that the consequences of certain destructive practices are clearly understood. Fear is fundamental to education; fear is fundamental to life.

Russell Kirk in a Chicago address based upon the text, "Fear of the Lord is the beginning of wisdom" (Ps. 111:10), said, "Without knowledge of fear we cannot know order in personality or society. Fear is an ineluctable part of the human condition. If fear is lacking, hope and aspirations fail. To demand from mankind freedom from fear as politically attainable was a silly piece of demagogic sophistry. If fear were wiped out altogether from our lives we would be desperately bored, longing for old or new terrors. There are things which rightfully we ought to fear if we are to enjoy any dignity as men. To fear to commit evil; to hate what is abominable, is the mark of manliness."

Then Kirk quotes a striking passage from George Shaw's book, *Back to Methusaleh*. "Good-natured, unambitious men are cowards when they have no religion. At the spectacle of half of Europe being kicked to death by the other half they stare in helpless horror, or are persuaded by the newspapers that this is a sound commercial investment and an act of Divine justice. They [good-natured, unambitious men without religion] are dominated and exploited, not only by greedy and often half-witted and half-alive weaklings who will do anything for cigars, champagne and motor cars and the more childish and selfish uses of money, but by able and sound administrators who can do nothing else with them than dominate and exploit them. Government and exploitation become synonymous under such circumstances, and the world is finally ruled by the childish, the brigands and the blackguards."[2]

Kirk continues, "Freedom from fear if I read St. John aright, is one of the planks in the platform of the anti-Christ. Such freedom is purchased only at the cost of spiritual and political enslavement. It ends at Armageddon. Lacking conviction that 'the fear of the Lord is the beginning of wisdom' the captains and kings yield to the fierce ideologues, the merciless adventurers, the charlatans, and the metaphysically mad, and then truly when the stern, righteous God of fear and love has been denied, the savage god lays down his new commandments. Yes, from the post-Christian church [Kirk is referring to the contemporary church] the dusty fear of God and the odor of sanctity have been quite cleansed. Within the doors there remains, spiritually speaking, simply a vacuum which nature abhors. Presently something will fill that vacuum, perhaps a rough beast, its hour come round at last, with a stench of death in its fur."

Men who fear God face life fearlessly. Men who do not fear God end up fearing everything.

Jesus said that we are to fear. Whom are we to fear? What are we to fear? He said, "Fear not them which kill the body, but are not able to kill the soul: but rather fear him which is able to destroy both soul and body in hell" (Matt. 10:28). This admonition was spoken in the context of persecution. "Behold," Jesus said to His disciples, "I send you forth as sheep in the midst of wolves. . . . They will deliver you up to the councils and they will scourge you in their synagogues; . . . and ye shall be hated of all men for my name's sake" (10:17-22); but, said Jesus, do not fear them. Do not be afraid of them! "Fear not them that can destroy the body but not the soul."

Does this mean therefore that Jesus was indifferent to the physical welfare of men? The question is almost sacrilegious, and its answer is superfluous. Who cared

more, did more for men's bodies? Never
has there been another like the Great Physician, the paragon of compassion and
love, filled with gentleness, tenderness,
caring.

Does this mean that the church is to
be indifferent to the physical welfare of
men? The answer is obvious. Wherever
the church has gone with the gospel of
Christ she has brought enlightenment,
compassion and healing. The church has
led in giving the world schools and col-
leges, progressive agricultural methods,
hospitals, clinics, orphanages, widows'
homes and care for the aging. Like rivers
of compassion the mission of the church
has flowed into valleys of need the world
around, over and over, age after age. Centuries before anybody ever thought of foreign aid or a Peace Corps the church was
there meeting and ministering to the
bodies and minds of men; and she continues her work throughout the world to
this very moment.

The church is busy by day and by night
binding the wounds of the terribly
bruised and burdened and broken in our
inner cities. Not as much as she should—
but she is there and must increase her
ministry there. The church is caring for

the orphans and the widows, the hungry
and the homeless and the hopeless in
Southeast Asia, Africa and Latin America.
Jesus was not indifferent to physical suffering, nor is His church. The church that
is faithful to the gospel does not ignore
the physical sufferings of men. The gospel
is for the whole person.

But Jesus did teach that the antidote
to irrational and unnecessary fear is a
greater fear, a basic fear. Who is to be
feared? Now at this point scholarship is
divided on the text. Some say the "him" in
verse 28—"Fear him who is able to destroy
both soul and body in hell"—refers to the
devil, on the grounds that the verses following, 29 through 31, in which Jesus
speaks of the loving concern of the Father,
would be out of place if God were the One
to be feared. Others argue that it is God
who is to be feared, and insist that the following verses give the reasons why He
ought to be feared. As the psalmist said,
"The fear of the Lord is the beginning of
wisdom." Even though the one to be
feared may not be absolutely clear in the
text, there is no doubt at all as to *what* is
to be feared: the destruction of the soul
and body in hell. Jesus is saying, according to one commentator, "Fear not the

persecutor but the tempter. Don't be afraid of the man who kills you for your fidelity, but fear the man who wants to buy you off, and the devil whose agent he is." Jesus is arguing for the incalculable value of one soul. "What shall it profit a man if he should gain the whole world and lose his own soul?" (Matt. 16:26). What have we done for a man after all if we feed him and clothe him and let him go to hell? No evil that befalls man this side of the grave can be compared with the destiny, the awful, indescribable destiny that awaits the unredeemed man beyond the grave.

Contemporary man finds the concept of hell, eternal judgment, the wrath of God to be archaic. In his sophistication he relegates such ideas to the realm of the superstitious, unworthy of rational consideration. But such conclusions must be weighed in the light of certain stubborn, irresistible data. Jesus took these matters seriously. Every record of His life and teaching indicates these subjects to be His preoccupation. So seriously did He take them that He submitted to an early death by crucifixion when He could have avoided it by repudiating His message. The apostles, who continued what Jesus began, took these matters seriously. And their teaching started a movement which has continued and grown for 2,000 years and is expanding faster than the population in Africa, South America and some parts of Asia today. That which Jesus began and His apostles continued is far and away the most powerful and influential force in human history. Despite all the effort that has been made to destroy the church, she exists today, 2,000 years since her inception, stronger than ever. Christ promised, "I will build my church and the gates of hell shall not prevail against her" (Matt. 16:18).

Furthermore, the Bible takes these matters seriously. The Bible is an ancient book, but year after year it outsells every modern best-seller. Though the Bible was completed nineteen centuries ago, it has been translated into more languages (more than 1,800) than any other book ever written. Its enemies have tried to destroy the Bible literally by confiscation and burning. Some of the brightest minds humanity has produced, involving the most brilliant scholarship, have attempted to discredit the Bible generation after generation. Yet the Bible remains the most read book, the most carefully studied book in the twentieth century. Last year more than 500 million, repeat *500 million*, copies of the Bible were published and sold. No other book has ever come close in its lifetime. The Bible does this annually.

It is hardly intelligent to disregard the teaching of Jesus which has persevered despite incredible opposition and hostility in every generation for two millenniums. Indifference to these stubborn facts is unworthy of thoughtful people.

Modern man is discovering the emptiness, the hollowness, the meaninglessness of life without an eternal reference. In a culture which caters to the body in every conceivable way, he is discovering that preoccupation with bodily appetites does not satisfy, is not fulfilling. The consummate product of the "liberated" man is a jaded, bored, fed up, exhausted culture, seeking for "kicks" in the most ancient of corrupt life-styles and practices. Modern man is discovering that nothing works right when God is rejected, when man becomes his own god and he finds no sustenance for his indestructible soul. Man is an eternal creature, made for eternity, and he is never satisfied with anything less. There is something basic to humanness that cannot be satisfied by anything tangible, material, visible. Humanness is spiritual as well as physical and will never be satisfied with that which gives only biological satisfaction.

The absolute moral law of God is no more to be ignored than the law of gravity. Violation of either ends in destruction, however clever the violation may be in man's self-justification.

Jesus said, "So shall it be at the end of the age. The angels shall come forth and sever the wicked from among the just, and shall cast them into the furnace of fire [that is, Gehenna; Jesus uses the word *hell* not *hades* in this text], and there shall be weeping and gnashing of teeth" (Matt. 13:40-42). Jesus said, "Then shall he say also unto them on the left hand, Depart from me, ye cursed, into everlasting fire, prepared for the devil and his angels. . . . These shall go away into everlasting punishment" (Matt. 25:41,46). Jesus said, "It is better for thee to enter into life maimed than having two hands to go into hell, into the fire, that never shall be quenched" (Matt. 18:8).

Paul said, "[They] shall be punished with everlasting destruction from the presence of the Lord and from the glory of his power" (2 Thess. 1:9). In Revelation we read, "The same shall drink of the wine of the wrath of God, which is poured out without mixture into the cup of his indignation; and he shall be tormented with fire and brimstone" (14:10); "The devil that deceived them was cast into the lake of fire and brimstone, where the beast and the false prophet are, and shall be tormented day and night for ever and ever. . . . And whosoever was not found written in the book of life was cast into the lake of fire. . . . But the fearful, and unbelieving, and the abominable, and murderers, and whoremongers, and sorcerers, and idolaters, and all liars, shall have their part in the lake which burneth with fire and brimstone: which is the second death" (20:10,15; 21:8).

Can you think of any leader you would trust more than one who was motivated by a healthy fear of or reverence for Almighty God and the eternally destructive power of evil? Or can you think of anything worse than a church or a Christian—warned and informed of the destiny of the lost—that would ignore the salvation of men's souls in its preoccupation with sociological, economic and political concern? In the church, the gospel is always fundamentally relevant to life, both eternally and in the here and now.

In the matter of mission, the church of Jesus Christ is absolutely unique in history. She exists for the salvation of men's eternal souls. No other organization or institution has this mission. There are hundreds of organizations, in addition to government itself, which exist for the social welfare of men; and incidentally these organizations are manned in great part by church people and receive a great part of their financial support from church people. They are doing what they are designed to do, thank God. They are not intended, nor will they ever devote themselves to the eternal welfare of men's souls. If the church fails in its unique mission there is no organization that will fill the breech. If the church fails to labor for the eternal redemption of the souls of men, she is failing, whatever else she does. If the church is not primarily concerned with the destiny of men beyond the grave, she is defaulting, however busy she may be in her care and concern for men.

The key to the missionary message is the propitiation of Christ Jesus. Take any phase of Christ's work—the healing phase, the saving and sanctifying phase; there is nothing limitless about those. "The Lamb of God which taketh away the sin of the world!"—that is limitless. The missionary message is the limitless significance of Jesus. Christ as the propitiation for our sins, and a missionary is one who is soaked in that revelation.

The key to the missionary message is the remissionary aspect of Christ's life, not His kindness and His goodness, and His revealing of the Fatherhood of God; the great limitless significance is that He is the propitiation for our sins. The missionary message is not patriotic, it is irrespective of nations and of individuals, it is for the whole world.[3]

June 2, 1965

Forty-three years ago I was part of an enterprise that was then caring for over 100,000 orphaned Armenian and other children left destitute by World War I and the Turkish Massacres.

Last summer my wife and I revisited the scenes of this early work, now Soviet Armenia. You can understand my dismay in finding not a trace, not a memory, of this humanitarian work. No one we met had ever heard of the "Near East Relief." There was, however, a great deal heard about the "Liberation."

In asking why evidence of this great humanitarian effort had disappeared, like a stream flowing into a desert, I have concluded that it was the failure to heed the example of the apostles: it left the Word of God to serve tables. (Acts 6:2)[4]

Humanitarianism is not Christianity. As high as the heaven is above the earth, so high is Christianity above humanitarianism. If we are not trying to snatch men from hell as brands from the burning then we are out of line with the mission of our Lord and disobedient to the mandate He gave His church. Hell is the ultimate enemy of men. The church is in the world to warn men of this and to point them to the Saviour who died for their sakes to save them from hell! This is relevant.

For the love of Christ constraineth us; because we thus judge, that if one died for all, then were all dead: and that he died for all, that they which live should not henceforth live unto themselves, but unto him which died for them, and rose again.

Wherefore henceforth know we no man after the flesh: yea, though we have known Christ after the flesh, yet now henceforth know we him no more.

Therefore if any man be in Christ, he is a new creature: old things are passed away; behold, all things are become new.

And all things are of God, who hath reconciled us to himself by Jesus Christ, and hath given to us the ministry of reconciliation; to wit, that God was in Christ, reconciling the world unto himself, not imputing their trespasses unto them; and hath committed unto us the word of reconciliation.

Now then we are ambassadors for Christ, as though God did beseech you by us: we pray you in Christ's stead, be ye reconciled to God. For he hath made him to be sin for us, who knew no sin; that we might be made the righteousness of God in him.

2 Corinthians 5:14-21

Chapter 4

Mission—Reconciliation

Should you attempt to reduce to one word the problems of history and our contemporary dilemma, you could not find a better word than *rift*. We live in a fragmented world, as though some cosmic giant had taken this ball we call earth and hurled it against some great mass, smashing it in pieces. We live in a broken world:

Internationally. Two great power blocs in mortal conflict, grinding between them many small nations struggling for neutrality and independence. There are two Germanys, two Koreas, two Chinas, two Europes, two Asias, two Africas.

Racially. We of course are very conscious of the rift between the blacks, Hispanics, native Americans and whites in America, but every nation suffers this rift between its peoples.

Economically. There are the desperately poor and the exorbitantly rich and affluent, the haves and the have-nots.

Intellectually. Multiplied millions remain illiterate coincident with an unprecedented explosion of knowledge.

Industrially. The labor-management rift, still a problem in America, is fast emerging in other nations of the world.

Domestically. We see the disintegration of the family through alienation between parents and children, between husbands and wives.

And perhaps worst of all, there is the rift within *man himself*; fragmented personalities, a devastating civil war within men producing anxieties and fears, neuroses and psychoses.

Even the *church* is fragmented, and today as rarely in history she suffers relentless tension.

Here is a problem of relevance. What is the answer to this broken world? Where is there healing for this earth rent by schism? The Bible answer, the intelligent answer, the one adequate answer can also be summed up in a word: *reconciliation*. The Bible reveals that the fundamental rift in history, producing all other divisions, is alienation between man and God. Man voluntarily alienated from God is disoriented in the world God created to be his home. Lost and disoriented, man is out of gear with God's order; therefore he does not mesh with his fellowmen, individually or corporately.

To meet this tragic rift in humanity's world, God has addressed Himself in the person of His Son, Jesus Christ. In the words of the text, "God was in Christ, reconciling the world to Himself" (2 Cor. 5:19). Paul records in another place, "God has made known to us in all wisdom and insight the mystery of His will, according to His purpose which He set forth in Christ as a plan for the fullness of time, to unite all things in Christ" (Eph. 1:9,10). And, "Through Christ God purposes to reconcile all things to Himself, making peace by the blood of His cross" (Col. 1:20).

Paul's statement in 2 Corinthians 5:14-21 sums up thoroughly the mission of Jesus Christ in the world, and the mandate He gave His church. All Christian responsibility and mission begin here. This is basic to the relevance of the church to the world. Christians are to be agents of reconciliation. Paul says, "All things are of God, who has reconciled us to Himself by Jesus Christ, and has given to us the ministry of reconciliation; to wit, that God was in Christ reconciling the world to Himself, not imputing unto them their trespasses and sins, and has committed unto us the word of reconciliation."

God has given to us the "ministry of reconciliation"; God has committed to us the "word of reconciliation." The ministry of reconciliation and the word of reconciliation are our inescapable mandate. Our lives, individually and collectively as people of God, must square with this commission if we are to be true to Christ. To make it very personal, do you have a disruptive influence where you are, or do you bring peace? Do you bring division or do you unite? Do you alienate or do you reconcile? Does your life have a unifying, reconciling, uniting influence, or does it have an alienating, disruptive, dis-peaceful influence? Do you bring peace or do you bring strife as a person?

What is the word of reconciliation?

What is essential to the understanding of this text? Unfortunately, this passage in 2 Corinthians has been one of the most misused and abused in the Bible. In the name of relevance men have used this passage to justify programs designed only to reconcile man with man while, at the same time, ignoring evangelism and the explicit purpose of reconciling man to God. Again and again one hears this passage referred to as grounds for purely humanitarian or sociological movements in the name of relevance, thereby rendering it utterly irrelevant. The reconciliation spoken of here does not stop with individual redemption or salvation, but it begins there. All Christian sociology and ethics begin with man's rightness with God through the blood of Jesus Christ His Son, according to Paul. If men are to be reconciled to each other ultimately, they first must be reconciled to God individually. On the other hand, individual salvation which does not issue in authentic social responsibility is sub-Christian.

The Word of Reconciliation

What is the word of reconciliation? In the first place Paul says, "We thus judge if one died for all, then we are all dead, and that He died for all that they which live should not henceforth live unto themselves, but unto Him which died and rose again" (2 Cor. 5:14,15). This is the word of reconciliation: Christ died, Christ rose. Note the context of this passage. Paul begins chapter 5 with a gracious, thrilling prospect beyond the grave. "While we are at home in the body we are absent from the Lord,. . . absent from the body and home with the Lord" (vv. 6,8). Then he discusses the very passion of his own life: he labors "to be accepted of the Lord" (v. 9). He speaks of the certainty of judgment (v. 10). He speaks of "the terror of the Lord" (v. 11) which he says compels him to persuade men to be reconciled to God. This is the word of reconciliation.

Also in this text Paul says, "Therefore if any man be in Christ he is a new creature. Old things are passed away, behold all things are become new" (v. 17). This is the word of reconciliation—the promise of a changed human nature, power that can transform human nature from selfishness to selflessness; from self-seeking to self-sacrificing. This cannot be legislated. This cannot be done by social structures. It has been tried; it breaks down because of the stubborn fact of pride or selfishness in the human heart. As one man put it, "No matter how cleverly you organize bad eggs, you can't get a good omelet."

Paul, constrained by God to go to this city of sin, Corinth—the wickedest city in one of the most depraved cultures in history—faced the deplorable social and moral conditions there in this conviction: "When I came to you, brethren, I came not with excellency of speech or of wisdom, declaring unto you the testimony of God. For I determined not to know anything among you, save Jesus Christ, and Him crucified" (1 Cor. 2:1,2). So far as this brilliant Jew was concerned, relevance to Corinthian evil meant Christ crucified. Why? Jesus said, "It is not that which goes into the man that defiles the man. It is what comes out of the man that defiles the man" (Matt. 15:17,18). And then He added, when His disciples asked Him to amplify, that everything which defiles human nature has its origin inside the human heart. It isn't how you organize human nature; it is something inside human nature that is the problem.

In an address which Albert Einstein made in 1948 he said, "I do not fear the explosive power of the atom bomb. What I fear is the explosive power of evil in the human heart." What is the answer to the explosive power of evil in the human heart? Where is the answer to that within man which defiles humanity? Jesus Christ and Him crucified! This is the word of reconciliation. This is the relevance of Christ. The gospel when believed (received) dissolves enmity in the heart and replaces it with love.

On the occasion of one of Chuck Colson's Prison Fellowship seminars in Washington, one of the prisoners was a former Ku Klux Klan leader from Mississippi. He had been sentenced to a long prison term for bombing a Jewish home. He despised blacks and Jews and Catholics with a vengeance in his pre-prison days. At dinner one evening he was introduced to Eldridge Cleaver, the black revolutionary activist who was an avowed Marxist before his encounter with Christ. That evening Chuck Colson, Harold Hughes, whom Colson had blacklisted as an enemy in former days, Tommy Tarrants, the former Ku Klux Klan leader who had received Christ in prison, and Eldridge Cleaver knelt together in prayer, their arms around each other. When men are reconciled to God, they find peace with one another.

Also in 2 Corinthians 5 Paul wrote, "God was in Christ, reconciling the world unto himself, not imputing their trespasses unto them" (v. 19). This is the word of reconciliation, forgiveness of sin through the blood of Christ's cross.

Someone has said guilt is the most corrosive influence in life. Who can measure the inefficiency due to guilt? The breakdown of human machinery caused by guilt? Think of the multiplied millions of dollars spent to resolve the problem of guilt.

Talk about relevance! Here it is, "God has made Christ to be sin for us, though He knew no sin, that we might be made the righteousness of God in Him" (v. 21). God reconciles men unto Himself, "not imputing their trespasses against them" (v. 19). Absolutely incredible! This is the sure word of reconciliation. This is truly relevance.

Finally, who is to be reconciled to whom? "As though God did beseech you by us, we pray you in Christ's stead be reconciled to God" (v. 20). This is the word of reconciliation, "Be reconciled to God." This is the authentic Christian message—the central thrust of the church's word to the world—be reconciled to God!

The Ministry of Reconciliation

What is the ministry of reconciliation? "Now then we are ambassadors for Christ" (v. 20). This involves selflessness. We do not represent ourselves! Wherever we are, wherever we go we represent our Lord. Paul says, "We commend not ourselves unto you." We bear His message, His word; there is nothing unilateral in our mission. We are in the world on God's behalf, among those who are alien to God. We are to obey orders from headquarters. We ought to dig into our diplomatic pouch every morning to get our directions.

Being an ambassador involves *diplomacy*, protocol. It has been disturbing to me through the years to observe how difficult it is for some Christians to honor others. They seem congenitally or constitutionally incapable of it. They may justify it by saying James exhorts us to not be a respecter of persons, and God is impartial; but Paul commands, "Honor to whom honor is due" (Rom. 13:7). I may not like the man, but I honor his office. I may not like the man, but I honor his uniform, the stars he wears as a general. Being an ambassador of Jesus Christ involves protocol. Diplomacy involves courtesy, common courtesy for the sake of Christ.

Being an ambassador involves *subtlety*, "Wise as serpents, harmless as doves" (Matt. 10:16). It involves faithfulness to our citizenship in heaven. It means we are in the world to represent the best interests of our Lord. Some of us are so undiplomatic, so obvious, so naive, so violent, so arbitrary, so inflexible, so self-willed. God gave us the softness and the toughness good diplomacy requires.

Being an ambassador of Christ involves *tension*. We stand between two worlds, two alienated worlds. Often there is militant opposition to Christ's kingdom. Some of us are tempted to withdraw, to lay down arms, to isolate ourselves from this troubled world, to insulate ourselves against its tragedy, to ignore the live issues which keep our world in constant ferment. But these issues will not go away. They are here. They are real. They are facts of life. They must be faced in Christ's strength and wisdom.

Who are the ambassadors? We who have been reconciled. "All things are of God, who has reconciled us unto Himself, and has given to us [reconciled ones] the ministry of reconciliation," who "has committed unto us [reconciled ones] the word of reconciliation" (2 Cor. 5:18,19). We who have been made new creatures in Christ, who have been born again, born of God; we who have been twice-born are the ambassadors, which, incidentally, is one explanation for the rift in the church and her failure in the world: members, enrolled in churches, who are unchanged, unregenerate, unreconciled, who have not been born again.

What is required of us ambassadors? Paul reminds us, "He died for all, that they which live should not henceforth live unto themselves, but unto Him who died for them, and rose again" (v. 15). This is very plain language. In the light of this requirement it is not difficult to understand the powerlessness of the church in the world. How pathetically self-centered we are. How desperately self-seeking. How defensive of self. How protective of self. How ambitious for self. Think what would happen if every Christian really gave himself away to Christ and began to live not for himself but for his Lord, who, "though He was in the form of God, thought it not something to be held onto but emptied Himself [made Himself of no reputation], became a servant and was obedient unto the death, even the death of the cross" (Phil. 2:6-8).

Crossless Christianity is powerless Christianity. Where there is no cross there is no power. Indeed where there is no cross there is no resurrection. Power involves sacrifice. Self-sacrifice. Much easier to sacrifice things than it is to sacrifice self. We are losing because we are struggling so hard to keep what we have and get more. We are forfeiting all we hold precious because we are striving interminably to guard it for ourselves. Jesus said, "He that seeks his life shall lose it. He that loses his life for my sake shall find it" (Matt. 16:25). Jesus said, "If any man will be my disciple let him deny himself and take up his cross daily and follow me" (16:24). This is relevance.

This message is meaningful only as each of us takes it seriously for himself. You do not have to accept this message. You can reject it, that is your prerogative; but you will never be a disciple of Christ if you do. You will be a part of the problem in our world, not a part of the answer. This ministry, this mission, is binding upon every one of us who professes to be Christian. That is very clear in the Scriptures. Think of the potential if each of us goes forth wherever duty calls—today, tomorrow—as an ambassador for Christ; living for Christ, not for ourselves; determined in His grace to be a reconciling influence, a redemptive force. Think of it! May God make us this kind of a people.

While Peter thought on the vision, the Spirit said unto him, Behold, three men seek thee. Arise therefore, and get thee down, and go with them, doubting nothing: for I have sent them.

Then Peter went down to the men which were sent unto him from Cornelius; and said, Behold, I am he whom ye seek: what is the cause wherefore ye are come?

And they said, Cornelius the centurion, a just man, and one that feareth God, and of good report among all the nation of the Jews, was warned from God by an holy angel to send for thee into his house, and to hear words of thee.

Then called he them in, and lodged them. And on the morrow Peter went away with them, and certain brethren from Joppa accompanied him.

And the morrow after they entered into Caesarea. And Cornelius waited for them, and had called together his kinsmen and near friends. And as Peter was coming in, Cornelius met him, and fell down at his feet, and worshipped him. But Peter took him up, saying, Stand up; I myself also am a man. And as he talked with him, he went in, and found many that were come together. And he said unto them, Ye know how that it is an unlawful thing for a man that is a Jew to keep company, or come unto one of another nation; but God hath shewed me that I should not call any man common or unclean. Therefore came I unto you without gainsaying, as soon as I was sent for: I ask therefore for what intent ye have sent for me?

And Cornelius said,. . . Now therefore are we all here present before God, to hear all things that are commanded thee of God.

Then Peter opened his mouth, and said, Of a truth I perceive that God is no respecter of persons: But in every nation he that feareth him, and worketh righteousness, is accepted with him.

Acts 10:19-35

Chapter 5

Jesus and Race Prejudice

Y ou cannot discuss Christian relevance without talking about people.
There are two great commandments
upon which, we are told by Jesus, "hang
all the law and the prophets": "Thou shalt
love the Lord thy God with all thy heart,
and with all thy soul, and with all thy
mind. This is the first and great commandment. And the second is like unto it,
Thou shalt love thy neighbor as thyself"
(Matt. 22:37-40).

The Apostle Paul wrote to the Romans,
"For this, Thou shalt not commit adultery, Thou shalt not kill, Thou shalt not
steal, Thou shalt not bear false witness,

Thou shalt not covet; and if there be any other commandment, it is briefly comprehended in this saying, namely, Thou shalt love thy neighbor as thyself. Love worketh no ill to his neighbour: therefore love is the fulfilling of the law" (Rom. 13:9,10).

The beloved Apostle John declared in his first epistle, "Every one that loveth is born of God, and knoweth God. He that loveth not knoweth not God; for God is love. . . . If we love one another, God dwelleth in us, and his love is perfected in us" (1 John 4:7,8,12). And in his strongest words, "If a man say, I love God, and hateth his brother, he is a liar: for he that loveth not his brother whom he hath seen, how can he love God whom he hath not seen?" (1 John 4:20). Godliness issues in mutual respect and love. No fact is more manifest in the Scriptures. Christian faith dissolves human prejudice. Faith that does not do so, whatever its profession, is not just sub-Christian; it is a contradiction.

Peter's experience with Cornelius dramatizes this basic fruit of Christian faith, for it represents the surgery of the Spirit on the last vestige of racial prejudice in Peter's heart. Peter said, "You know that it is an unlawful thing for a man that is a Jew to keep company or come unto one of another nation" (Acts 10:28). Never has prejudice been more deeply imbedded in the human heart. History has never known stronger racial prejudice than Peter is talking about here. It is impossible for us today to imagine the contempt with which Jewry held the non-Jew in Peter's day. Juvenal says that the Jews were taught by Moses "not to show the way except to one who practices our rites, and to guide the circumcized alone to the well which they seek." They would not even give directions to a non-Jew. Tacitus said of the Jew that "among themselves they are inflexibly faithful and ready with charitable aid, but hate all others as enemies. They keep separate from all strangers in eating, sleeping and matrimonial connections." Edersheim, in his *Jewish Social Life*, says that "on coming from the market an orthodox Jew was expected to immerse himself to avoid defilement." He might not enter the house of a Gentile, for "he looked upon it to be ceremonially polluted." The Gentile was an abomination. His touch was defiled; his customs were abhorrent; his religion was a blasphemy.

One interesting fact about this is that

there is no Old Testament regulation forbidding such social contact. These regulations were added by the rabbis and became binding by social custom. Here is an insight into the human tendency to reduce authentic faith to the traditions of men and to social custom, thereby in effect arriving at a Godless religion which has all the form but none of the substance. In the words of Jesus, "Well hath Isaiah prophesied of you hypocrites, as it is written, 'This people honoreth me with their lips, but their heart is far from me. In vain do they worship me, teaching for doctrines the commandments of men. For laying aside the commandment of God you hold the tradition of men. . . . You have a fine way of rejecting the commandments of God that you may keep your own tradition' " (Mark 7:6-9).

Peter was committed to this tradition. He said, "It is an unlawful thing for a man that is a Jew to keep company or to come to one of another nation." Hence the possibility of an apartheid policy based upon human tradition which has been elevated to the status of divine authority. It is not uncommon to hear segregation defended on what is assumed to be biblical grounds; and thus, to her terrible shame,

the church has been called the most seg-
regated institution in America!

But Peter had come a long way by this
time. He had heard himself (I say that
advisedly because he seems to have
received his message direct from the
Spirit) at Pentecost, he had heard himself
say as he preached on that unforgettable
day, "And it shall come to pass in the last
days, saith God, I will pour out of my
Spirit upon all flesh . . . and it shall come
to pass, that whosoever shall call on the
name of the Lord shall be saved" (Acts
2:17,21).

Peter knew of the great spiritual awak-
ening which had come to the despised
Samaritans through the anointed preaching of Philip. He was, in fact, at the time of
this experience, dwelling in the home of
one whose vocation was held in contempt
but who must have been a brother in
Christ—Simon the tanner, in Joppa. The
trade of a tanner was held in such
supreme contempt that if a girl was
betrothed to a tanner without knowing he
followed that calling the betrothal was
void. A tanner had to build his house fifty
cubits outside the city. Nevertheless, even
though Peter had been baptized with the
Holy Spirit, had preached that Pentecostal

sermon, knew of the revival in Samaria, and now dwelt with a tanner, an extraordinary act of God was required to break the back of prejudice in his life.

Peter was on the housetop praying at the ninth hour, mid-afternoon; he was hungry; he fell into a trance. It was as though "heaven was opened and a great sheet knit at the four corners was let down to earth wherein were all manner of fourfooted beasts of the earth, and wild beasts, and creeping things, and fowls of the air. And a voice from heaven said, 'Rise, Peter; kill and eat' " (Acts 10:11-13). Now God had given the Jews very strict rules concerning their eating habits. Obviously they could not eat the food served by non-Jews, but they had projected this beyond food to the non-Jews themselves, and considered them to be unclean. Observe the tremendous and inflexible hold religious tradition can get on a man. Peter responded to the command, "Not so, Lord" (v. 14). Religious tradition can even make a man say no to God! Religious tradition, without the love of God, can become the most intolerable influence in life. In Acts 11, verses 2 and 3, it is recorded, "When Peter was come up to Jerusalem, they that were of the cir-

cumcision contended with him, saying,
Thou wentest in to men uncircumcised,
and didst eat with them.' "

Then, of course, there was the element
of self-righteousness and pride. Peter said
to the Lord, "I have never eaten anything
that is common or unclean." God's
answer to Peter's obstinance was, "What
God hath cleansed, that call not thou
common" (vv. 8,9). Three times did God
do this, leaving Peter puzzled as to its significance, but he would soon be enlight-
ened.

The lesson Peter learned, and which
was transmitted to the apostolic church,
leaves no ambiguity: "God hath shewed
me that I should not call any man common or unclean. . . . Of a truth I perceive
that God is no respecter of persons: but in
every nation he that feareth him, and
worketh righteousness, is accepted with
him" (10:28,34,35). This is the glorious
fact about the true church of Christ. This
is the thrilling relevance about authentic
Christian faith. All races and colors and
languages are united in Christ, in one
inseparable, indivisible bond of love and
mission. Paul wrote to the Galatians,
"There is neither Jew nor Greek, there is
neither bond nor free, there is neither

male nor female: for ye are all one in Christ Jesus" (Gal. 3:28). To the Colossians, "There is neither Greek nor Jew, circumcision nor uncircumcision, Barbarian, Scythian, bond nor free: but Christ is all, and in all" (Col. 3:11).

This is not just a sociological or humanitarian matter. This is a Christian issue, a decidedly spiritual matter with eternal significance. Peter had to learn, as did his Jewish brethren in the apostolic church, that God's redemptive purpose was not exclusive, but universal. It was not nationalistic but worldwide. It was for all men: "Whosoever shall call upon the name of the Lord" (Acts 2:21). It is fairly obvious that the apostolic church learned that lesson. The deplorable tragedy is that the church in subsequent generations could so easily unlearn and become as prejudiced and inflexible and obstinate as Peter and his colleagues were in that first generation. Hence the accusation by the world that the church is irrelevant.

Now if you have been angered by this message, or disturbed, or if at this moment you resent the writer, I urge you openly to seek God's will for yourself concerning this. This is not something to criticize the church about; this is some-

thing about which to examine your own
conscience before the clear teaching of the
Word of God! If you have trouble with this
teaching because of your background, the
culture in which you have been reared—
traditions and customs—just remember
Peter and ask Christ to help you. The
Word is very clear. "God is not a respecter
of persons." No man is to be called common or unclean. Whosoever is born of God
loves. He that loves not knows not God, for
God is love. We have committed to us the
mission of reconciliation; we have been
ordained to be ambassadors for Christ.
What an exciting prospect is ours today
when race is such a potent, explosive
issue worldwide, to prove the authenticity
of our faith by our love for all, and our
acceptance of all who are acceptable with
God. Whatever our attitude toward
marches and demonstrations is beside
the point; the real test is our relationship
with others personally. This is our grand
challenge, I believe, in the name of Christ
and for the sake of His kingdom and lost
men. God help us, each of us, to take it
seriously in obedience and love. This is
relevance.

And, behold, a certain lawyer stood up, and tempted him, saying, Master, what shall I do to inherit eternal life?

He said unto him, What is written in the law? how readest thou?

And he answering said, Thou shalt love the Lord thy God with all thy heart, and with all thy soul, and with all thy strength, and with all thy mind; and thy neighbour as thyself.

And he said unto him, Thou hast answered right: this do, and thou shalt live.

But he, willing to justify himself, said unto Jesus, And who is my neighbour?

And Jesus answering said, A certain man went down from Jerusalem to Jericho, and fell among thieves, which stripped him of his raiment, and wounded him, and departed, leaving him half dead. And by chance there came down a certain priest that way: and when he saw him, he passed by on the other side. And likewise a Levite, when he was at the place, came and looked on him, and passed by on the other side. But a certain Samaritan, as he journeyed, came where he was: and when he saw him, he had compassion on him, and went to him, and bound up his wounds, pouring in oil and wine, and set him on his own beast, and brought him to an inn, and took care of him.

And on the morrow when he departed, he took out two pence, and gave them to the host, and said unto him, Take care of him; and whatsoever thou spendest more, when I come again, I will repay thee.

Which now of these three, thinkest thou, was neighbour unto him that fell among the thieves?

And he said, He that shewed mercy on him. Then said Jesus unto him, Go, and do thou likewise.

Luke 10:25-37

Chapter 6

Gracious Neighbor

The trouble is not that Christianity is not relevant, but that Christians so often give the impression of irrelevance. The gospel has not failed; we have failed in our presentation—our demonstration. The breakdown is at the level of communication—of action.

This writing is based on the conviction that the historic apostolic faith is relevant to the fundamental need of human nature in this generation, all past generations, and all future generations. That the *kerygma*, which is the Greek word for the oral tradition—that is the gospel as preached by Peter and Paul, James and

John, indeed the message of all the apostles, now faithfully recorded in the twenty-seven books of the New Testament, and implicit in the thirty-nine books of the Old Testament—is literally Almighty God's unique, timeless, and completely adequate solution to the root cause of all human woe from the beginning of mankind to its consummation. That the message of the Old and New Testaments is an accurate, trustworthy record of man's perennial need and its remedy. That the Bible is the only infallible rule for faith and life, for all men everywhere, in all generations. That man-made remedies, however wise and clever their source and however relevant they may seem to be at the time, are always transient, always address themselves to the effect, never to the cause of the human dilemma, and therefore not only do not solve but actually compound the problem. That human wisdom, which proliferates these man-made solutions in its effort to improve upon the Bible, only obscures and emasculates the message. That though the remedy is one and changeless because the fundamental need is one and changeless, the communication of that remedy to those in need is as varied as those through whom God the

Holy Spirit works and witnesses redemptively.

The role of every Christian, every bona fide Christian—his sacred vocation—is to live and act in history redemptively in the power of the Holy Ghost and for the sake of Jesus Christ. He is in fact, if he is truly Christian, an ambassador of Christ, commending Him to a world that is mostly indifferent, disinterested, hostile, and universally in desperate need. In our modern, pragmatic world, conditioned as it is to the empirical method, the acid test for any claim is, Does it work? Demonstration is prerequisite to acceptance in contemporary culture. In this respect, incidentally, modern man is not unlike the Apostle Thomas who refused to believe in the resurrection of Jesus until he had received demonstrable proof. He said to the other disciples who had seen Jesus alive following His resurrection, "Except I shall see in his hands the print of the nails, and put my finger into the print of the nails, and thrust my hand into his side, I will not believe." Thomas got his satisfaction eight days later and responded to Jesus, "My Lord and my God" (John 20:25,28). Jesus never ignored the honest demand for proof, and authentic Christian faith has nothing to fear from the most critical demands of honest pragmatism. Indeed Jesus insisted, "If any man is willing to do, he shall know . . ." (see John 7:17).

In his book, *The New Reformation*, Bishop John A. T. Robinson quotes a pioneer contemporary missionary, Horace Simanowski, who labors among the working classes of western Germany. Simanowski said, "Previously the basic problem confronting man was how can I find a gracious God? This question drove men to search desperately for an answer. It was the motor for their action in the world. It unleashed crusades and wars. This cry robbed them of sleep. But we no longer ask this question, or we label it antiquated. But a different question haunts us also. It agitates entire nations. It makes us in our turn victims of anxiety and despair. The question is how can I find a gracious neighbor? How can we still somehow live in peace with one another?" Then Robinson continues, "There lies the difference. The Old Reformation revolved around Luther's agonized question and his triumphant, liberating answer, 'by faith alone.' The old Reformation released to men a gracious God, but the world today is not asking 'How can I find a gracious God,' it is asking, 'How can I find a gracious neighbor.' " This is an exceedingly stimulating thought, and it suggests a fundamental aspect of Christian witness in the world which Jesus vividly dramatized in the familiar parable of the Good Samaritan. We certainly know that, generally speaking, our modern world is not lying awake at night looking for a gracious God; in general it couldn't care less. But our modern world is languishing for gracious neighbors.

Read the parable again. "Jesus answering said, A certain man went down from Jerusalem to Jericho, and fell among thieves, which stripped him of his raiment and wounded him and departed, leaving him half dead. And by chance there came down a certain priest that way: and when he saw him, he passed by on the other side. And likewise a Levite, when he was at the place, came and looked on him, and passed by on the other side. But a certain Samaritan, as he journeyed, came where he was: and when he saw him, he had compassion on him, and went to him, and bound up his wounds, pouring in oil and wine, and set him on his own beast, and brought him to an inn,

and took care of him. And on the morrow
when he departed, he took out two pence,
and gave them to the host, and said unto
him, Take care of him; and whatsoever
thou spendest more, when I come again, I
will repay thee' " (Luke 10:30-35). Talk
about revolutionary teaching! So revolutionary that we find it very difficult to
accept, certainly to live by.

Think about this parable. "A certain
man"—Jesus deliberately gave this man
in need anonymity. It could have been
anyone. There was nothing about the
man which elicited aid except his need.
He had been beaten and robbed and left in
a ditch half dead. His dilemma was all that
qualified him. We do not know whether he
was a good man or a bad man, a religious
or a non-religious man. He was just someone in need. Jesus said, "By chance there
came down a certain priest that way: and
when he saw him, he passed by on the
other side. And likewise a Levite, when he
was at the place, came and looked on
him." (I wonder what he must have
thought as he looked at the suffering man
in the ditch.) He "looked on him, and
passed by on the other side." A priest and
a Levite. Both descendants of Levi, the
third son of Jacob. Priests were always

Levites, but Levites were not necessarily priests. Priests were chosen from among the Levites and consecrated to their holy office. All Levites were purified and were considered gifts to Aaron the high priest and his sons. Jesus' point is very clear. Those who personified the religion of Israel failed completely to communicate the love and mercy and compassion of the God they professed to serve. They were, in fact, a horrible misrepresentation, a tragic caricature of that for which their holy faith stood. They were the epitome of pious irrelevance. They were what Jesus referred to as salt without its savor, therefore good for nothing. They were good men, but they were good for nothing.

What a contrast the Samaritan. When he saw him "he had compassion on him and went to him and bound up his wounds, pouring in oil and wine, and set him on his own beast and brought him to the inn and took care of him. On the morrow when he departed he said to the host, as he gave him two pence, now you take care of him, and whatever you spend in his care, I will repay you when I return."

The occasion for this parable is significant. "And behold a certain lawyer stood up and tempted Jesus, saying, 'Master

what shall I do to inherit eternal life?' He said unto him, 'What is written in the law? How readest thou?' And he answering said, 'Thou shalt love the Lord thy God with all thy heart, and with all thy soul, and with all thy strength, and with all thy mind, and thy neighbor as thyself.' Jesus said unto him, 'Thou hast answered right, this do and thou shalt live.' But the lawyer, willing to justify himself, said unto Jesus, 'And who is my neighbor?' "
By the way, if this incident were lifted out of the New Testament and this encounter between a devoted Christian and a young professional man occurred today—with the professional man asking the devoted Christian—"What must I do to inherit eternal life?" if the Christian were to answer in the very words which Jesus used he would be completely indicted by certain people I know who are very articulate about a conventional witness. If anyone today talked to a man, as Jesus did, who was seeking eternal life, he would be highly criticized by many for his failure. It would be said of him, he did not witness the gospel.

To the question, "What must I do to inherit eternal life?" Jesus answered with a question, as He often did: "What is writ-

ten in the law? How do you read it?" The
lawyer replied, "Thou shalt love the Lord
thy God with all thy heart, and with all thy
soul, and with all thy strength, and with
all thy mind; and thy neighbor as thyself."
Jesus responded, "That is the right
answer. Do this, and you will live." If this
record can be trusted, and I believe it can,
this is the way Jesus talked to one man
seeking eternal life. What had begun as a
neat little trick to discredit Jesus ended
up with a trapped lawyer; so this very
sophisticated man tried to wiggle out of
his dilemma. "He, willing to justify himself . . . "—the *New English Bible* trans-
lates, "wanting to vindicate himself." How
human. How contemporary. How clever
we have become, with language, at rationalizing in order to vindicate disobedience.
We have mastered the art of rationalizing
so we can be comfortable Christians
instead of revolutionary as Christ was.
The lawyer, "wanting to vindicate himself," said unto Jesus, "And who is my
neighbor?" The way Jesus handled this
question is fundamental to Christian witness in this age or in any age.

Observe again the lawyer's question,
designed to get himself off the defensive:
"And who is my neighbor?" (It is quite

illuminating that he ignored completely the first commandment.) "Who is my neighbor?" He was asking for a simple formula whereby he would know whom he was supposed to love. As far as he was concerned the burden of proof rested with someone else. It was up to somebody else, somewhere, to prove he merited the lawyer's love. "Who is my neighbor?" Jesus turned the obligation completely around: the man in need was an unknown. The only thing that qualified him for help was his need, and when the story was finished Jesus drove the truth home with penetrating power. "Which now of these three, thinkest thou, was neighbour unto him that fell among the thieves?" He ignored the question, "Who is my neighbor?" Instead He asked, "Which one of these, the priest, the Levite or the Samaritan, was neighbor?" The burden of proof does not rest upon the one who is supposed to be loved; the burden of proof rests upon the lover. It was as though Jesus said, "Asking who is my neighbor is utterly irrelevant; you be neighbor to anybody in need, if you are there." Well the lawyer got the point, and Jesus made the final thrust, "Go, and do thou likewise."

Think of it. Think of it! All the law and

the prophets summed up in two commandments: love God; love your neighbor. The whole moral law of God comprehended in two simple precepts. All that God requires of man fulfilled in two uncomplicated duties: love God; love your neighbor. Now, of course, only Jesus Christ fulfilled this moral law, and because of everyone's failure—generation by generation—to love God and love his neighbor, history is filled with woe; humanity suffers indescribable tragedy; the world moves on into ever-increasing and compounded frustration, despite all its sophisticated, scientific, technological, intellectual efforts. To resolve this inexorable process in history, Jesus Christ, the perfect man, fulfilled the law to perfection, then laid down His life on the cross, suffering the long-term consequences of human failure and sin, and rose from the dead to bring the transforming power of eternal life to anyone who would receive it by faith.

If this is fulfilling of the law, and Jesus as well as Paul said it is, and if the same Jesus who fulfilled this law now dwells in us who are professed disciples of His, surely there ought to be some evidence of this compassion in us that was in Him.

Jesus was the gracious neighbor; Jesus was the personification of the Good Samaritan in the parable; Jesus was the incarnation of love for God and neighbor. However empirical and pragmatic our contemporary world, however indifferent or hostile to Jesus Christ and the gospel, the fact remains that the world in which we live is lost in loneliness and loveless-ness. It suffers alienation everywhere. Man is losing his identity. He is Mr. Anon-ymous. He is becoming a cipher in a meaningless world of computer systems. He languishes for a gracious neighbor.

The Incarnate Christ ascended to the right hand of the Father after He finished His earthly mission. He had commanded His disciples to wait for Pentecost, fifty days after His crucifixion. Nothing to do. Wait! No mission. Wait! Wait for the prom-ise. On that unforgettable day of Pente-cost, Jesus Christ sent the Holy Spirit into the world, into history, into the very bodies of believers to inhabit those bodies, that the Spirit of God might con-tinue the incarnate mission of Christ in us, now indwelt by Him! The true church is literally the incarnation of Jesus Christ in the world. Surely, whatever else we demonstrate to the world, we ought to manifest His love, His compassion.

John begins his Gospel with a so-called prologue. The first words are, "In the beginning was the Word, and the Word was with God and the Word was God." But apparently the Word was not enough even for God to communicate with men, because John adds, a few verses later, "And the Word was made flesh and dwelt among us,. . .full of grace and truth" (v. 14). The Word was made flesh. That is evangelical relevance! The world is not listening to our words today. It is looking for Love incarnate. Words are necessary; the gospel has to be told, heralded, preached. But words are not enough; our lives must literally be the incarnation of what we profess. That is God's way. That is the way of relevance today and in every age.

You heard the question which the lawyer asked Jesus. You heard Jesus' answer. You heard the lawyer's pathetic effort to get himself off the defensive. You heard the parable which Jesus told to this man who wanted to vindicate himself; and you heard the conclusion which the sacred record gives. This is God's word; this is binding upon you and me. "Go therefore and do thou likewise!"

Then came to him the mother of Zebedee's children with her sons, worshipping him, and desiring a certain thing of him. And he said unto her, What wilt thou? She saith unto him, Grant that these my two sons may sit, the one on thy right hand, and the other on the left, in thy kingdom.

But Jesus answered and said, Ye know not what ye ask. Are ye able to drink of the cup that I shall drink of, and to be baptized with the baptism that I am baptized with? They say unto him, We are able.

And he saith unto them, Ye shall drink indeed of my cup, and be baptized with the baptism that I am baptized with: but to sit on my right hand, and on my left, is not mine to give, but it shall be given to them for whom it is prepared of my Father.

And when the ten heard it, they were moved with indignation against the two brethren.

But Jesus called them unto him, and said, Ye know that the princes of the Gentiles excercise dominion over them, and they that are great exercise authority upon them. But it shall not be so among you: but whosoever will be great among you, let him be your minister; and whosoever will be chief among you, let him be your servant: even as the Son of man came not to be ministered unto, but to minister, and to give his life a ransom for many.

Matthew 20:20-28

Chapter 7

The Church in the World

Three texts—three images. A trilogy of texts, a trilogy of truths which suggest the authentic influence of the church in the world: *salt, light, servant.*

Salt—Matthew 5:13: "Ye are the salt of the earth; but if the salt has lost its taste, how shall its saltiness be restored? It is no longer good for anything except to be thrown out and trodden under foot of men." Here Jesus suggests the possibility of the good man who is good for nothing; good, but useless. The man who is so "heavenly minded he is no earthly good." He is salt without savor. Salt dissolves and disappears when it is serving its purpose. It is useless as long as it retains its identity in the saltshaker

Light—Matthew 5:14: "You are the light of the world. . . . Let your light so shine before men, that they may see your good works and give glory to your Father who is in heaven" (v. 16). (Note to whom the credit for good works accrues in the authentic Christian life.) Light is not for its own sake but to illuminate something else. One is most conscious of light when it is poor. When it illuminates properly, one is least aware of it. You do not look at light normally!

The ego which is the root of sin in individual man tends to be compounded in collective man. The ego which is such a problem to us as individual Christians tends to be a greater problem to our Christian institutions. The humility which ought to characterize the Christian ought to be true of his institutions as well. Think of the things that remain unfinished because somewhere along the line the initiator discovered he was not getting the recognition he felt he deserved, or the good things done which have been nullified because the doer demanded his reward. Paul, in describing the delicate interdependence of the church, wrote, "If one suffers—all suffer; if one is honored, all rejoice" (1 Cor. 12:26). We have this turned around: we suffer when another is honored, rejoice when he suffers. We need to learn to thank God when we do not get the credit for something we have done; or better still, to thank God when somebody else gets the credit for what we have done.

The church is suffering in the world today because of this institutional ego. She is demanding recognition. She is falsely preoccupied with her corporate image in society. She is being intimidated by the wisdom and the ways of men—suffering from an inferiority complex because she is being told that she has failed contemporary man. If she has failed, it is because she has abandoned the message and the ministry left her by Jesus Christ; she is embarrassed by her apostolic legacy, and in her lust for relevance has turned to the wisdom of this world to fight the sins of this world. She is jumping on the bandwagon of humanistic movements, trying to put in her "two-cents worth" and thereby tragically failing to be the unique redemptive force in history God intended. There is a basic sense in which the church, if she is true to herself, will never receive and ought not to expect recognition from the world. The world simply cannot begin to comprehend, let alone give the church credit commensurate with her value to the world. The Head of the church has never received this recognition. Why should we? The world crucified Him! What right have we to expect anything different?

We need to be committed to the ministry of anonymity! We need to have the mind of Christ as Paul describes it in Philippians 2:5-8. The true influence of the true church cannot be measured. It is immeasurable! It is not monolithic or massive. The maximum influence of the church is the aggregate of Spirit-filled, Christ-loving men and women, gathering for worship, instruction, fellowship and prayer—then dissolving into the society around them as a, what William James called, "benevolent infection." In nautical terms, there is a difference between a binnacle and a barnacle. The binnacle houses the light, the barnacle is an intruder—a foreign substance which attaches itself to the hull and becomes a burden. It must be removed sporadically. Our institutions ought to be binnacles, not barnacles.

Some generous, hospitable friend

invites you to a good steak dinner. You salt the steak and enjoy it. And when you have finished you think to yourself, and may remark to your fellow diners, "What a delicious steak." But you most certainly do not say, "My, wasn't that fine salt!"

Servant—Matthew 20:26-28: This ego, which is so prolific, expresses itself quite commonly in the desire to be served. (Which is probably the explanation for the indignation of the ten in the narrative, v. 24). In the conventional local structure of the church, a congregation calls a pastor to "serve" them. And they resent it—and are usually frank to let it be known—when the pastor does not so oblige. "Why didn't you call on me?" etc., etc., etc. There is a sense, of course, in which a pastor is a servant to servants, and he must never forget this—must never forget that humiliating experience of the disciples when their Lord girded Himself with a towel and washed their feet. But neither must the pastor forget that he is called to serve Christ and equip and lead the people he serves to serve Christ.

The extrovert God of John 3:16 does not beget an introvert people. There is a terrible tendency to make the gospel serve us, to use it as a protection against the realities of life as though Christ died to preserve the status quo—or to make us more comfortable—or just to make the world a better place in which to live. We must resist, with all the wisdom and strength God gives us, the diabolical temptation to force the gospel to identify with some human system, to make Christ the servant of some vested interest! "God so loved the world that he gave his only begotten Son that whosoever believeth on him should not perish but have everlasting life." If this God is in His church, this love will be manifest and the church will be constrained by this love to go out to that world, in love, with the message and the ministry of love. This is the work of the church; the work she has been left in the world to fulfill.

Unfortunately, though we have loudly professed our loyalty to His mandate, we have been inclined to deny it by our conventional practices. Let me illustrate this from my own experience.

When I began the ministry twenty-three years ago I had very strong convictions in this regard. Very strong, and very wrong! I believed in mission with a vengeance. But I planned and labored as though the work of the church consisted in the maintenance and prosperity of the establishment—and, incidentally, my personal success. (I would never have put it in those words then. I just operated on that basis.) The work of the church was what we did in the building and for the institution. In short the work of the church was the PROGRAM! In those days I had one simple criterion for a good church member and it was his involvement with the establishment: his attendance at stated meetings; his work for the building and the program. Obviously one who attended Sunday School, morning worship, Sunday evening groups, evening service and midweek prayer meeting was five times the Christian that the one who came only Sunday morning was. I actually resented all competition with community and civic organizations and, above all, other churches. (Of course, I tried my best to conceal this.) Everything outside MY church, including other Christian organizations, constituted a threat to my success. If P.T.A. met Wednesday evening it was understood that prayer meeting would be the choice of the "dedicated" Christian. It was unthinkable that a good member would let Rotary or Chamber of Commerce or a union meeting or school

function interfere with his proper "commitment."

What has been the result of this kind of
thinking and practice? The church suc-
ceeds in pulling Christians out of the
world, out of society, out of community
and civic affairs. It has become a little
island of irrelevant piety surrounded by
an ocean of need. And our preoccupation
with the establishment is so complete
that we cannot even see the ocean—
except, of course, as there is somebody
out there that we covet for the program.

The congregation has become an
exclusive little system of satellites orbiting
around the program—or perhaps it would
be more accurate and honest to say, orbiting around the pastor. Meanwhile, as the
church has defaulted, those "secular"
institutions out there in the community,
lacking leadership which takes God seriously, have turned themselves over to
those who have no interest or time for the
church. We have failed! Yet somehow we
have managed to blame other organizations and justify our own passion to be
served. Now we bemoan the fact that labor
unions, service clubs, chambers of commerce, school systems, and government
itself are so thoroughly secularized that

the church is on the outside, leaving the others without an influence.

The blasphemous contradiction of this concept began to dawn on me when I recognized the frustration of good men in the church with nothing to do. Hollywood Presbyterian Church, for example, where I served for nine years, had about seven thousand on the rolls but needed not more than four hundred to run its affairs. (Or the church I now serve with more than two thousand and only two hundred needed for the establishment. The sheer absurdity of this caricature of the work of the church comes to light when one sees how busy some pastors become trying to "find jobs" for members, and the best they can do is to challenge them to "come down to the church Tuesday evening and paint the chairs in the primary department.") Ministers became personnel managers or employment agents with the impossible (and irrelevant task) of trying to get everyone "busy" in the establishment.

It all came to a head in a dentist's chair. Dr. James Sheets, one of the finest young men in the Hollywood Presbyterian Church, sought my counsel as he worked on my teeth. He had been asked to be president of the school board of Inglewood, a responsibility which would force him to drop much of what he was doing in the church. Resentment burned within me at the audacity of a board of education robbing MY church of one of the finest leaders. Fortunately, I was unable to respond immediately due to the work on my teeth. When at last I could speak, the Spirit of God had dealt with me and I was able to say, "Jimmie, I can't imagine anything more wonderful than for a committed Christian like you to be president of a board of education." Think what it would mean if the boards of education in all our great cities were headed by Godly people who were servants of Christ!

The false dichotomy of sacred and secular is a great hindrance to Christian influence. And we must be dispossessed of the idea that the business of the church is sacred, but business downtown is secular; teaching the Bible is sacred, teaching in public schools is secular; worship is sacred, work is secular—except as it is done in the church. What of Jesus Himself? He was a carpenter's apprentice and master carpenter for at least half of His lifetime. Were only three years spent in sacred pursuits? The answer is painfully obvious! Everything Jesus did was sacred. All He did was for the Father's sake and to the Father's glory. He had come to do the Father's will and He made it clear, even at twelve years of age, that He must be "about His Father's business." Likewise the Apostle Paul exhorted, "Whatsoever you do, whether ye eat or drink, do all to the glory of God" (1 Cor. 10:31).

The work of the church is outside the establishment. Outside the church. In the world. And it takes every member to do it! Nowhere in the Bible is the world exhorted to "come to church." But the church's mandate is clear: she must go to the world. All that happens inside the institution is in order that the church may do her work outside. The measure of what takes place inside the sanctuary on Sunday is the measure of what happens when the sanctuary is empty Monday through Saturday, and the church is scattered, infiltrating all the social structures of the world. The work of the ministry belongs to the one in the pew, not the one in the pulpit (see Eph. 4:7,8,11,12), and it is the holy obligation of every member of the Body—wherever he is, whatever he is doing. He is called of God to be a witness for Christ in all of life. However he makes his living, his vocation is Christ's mission.

Two common questions with conventional and correct answers will illustrate this: (1) "Where is your church?" "5500 River Road, Washington, D.C." (2) "What does your church do?" "Oh, we are very busy. We really have a program—three services on Sunday; Sunday School for all ages; Sunday evening groups for all ages; midweek prayer meetings; and a very active youth program. We have fine choirs; faithful officers and committees; women's groups and men's groups. We are busy!" So the conventional answers go, indicating almost total preoccupation with the institution. But what ought the answer to be? (1) "Where is your church?" Answer: "She is all over metropolitan Washington; in about five hundred homes and apartments, in schools and clubs and markets and offices; in the Pentagon; on Capitol Hill; in government boards and agencies." (2) "What does your church do?" Answer: "Many things: she keeps house; teaches school; sells groceries and hardware, clothing and cars, insurance and appliances. She practices law and medicine and dentistry. She makes laws and serves in the military. She constructs highways and buildings, serves our government overseas in embassies, Peace Corps and Foreign Aid programs. She is everywhere, in everything, doing everything that needs doing for the sake of Christ, for the glory of God."

What an incredible privilege the pastor has facing such a congregation every Sunday! If he is faithful to his calling, he "equips the saints for the work of ministry," sends them out to the world, into all its institutions and structures—faithful ambassadors for Christ. This is his task. This is the challenge, the immeasurable opportunity incumbent upon every Christian.

Now Peter and John went up together into the temple at the hour of prayer, being the ninth hour. And a certain man lame from his mother's womb was carried, whom they laid daily at the gate of the temple which is called Beautiful, to ask alms of them that entered into the temple; who seeing Peter and John about to go into the temple asked an alms.

And Peter, fastening his eyes upon him with John, said, Look on us.

And he gave heed unto them, expecting to receive something of them.

Then Peter said, Silver and gold have I none; but such as I have give I thee: In the name of Jesus Christ of Nazareth rise up and walk. And he took him by the right hand, and lifted him up: and immediately his feet and ankle bones received strength. And he leaping up stood, and walked, and entered with them into the temple, walking, and leaping, and praising God.

And all the people saw him walking and praising God: and they knew that it was he which sat for alms at the Beautiful gate of the temple: and they were filled with wonder and amazement at that which had happened unto him.

And as the lame man which was healed held Peter and John, all the people ran together unto them in the porch that is called Solomon's, greatly wondering.

Acts 3:1-11

Chapter 8

As I Have I Give

The healing of the lame man is a very familiar incident in the New Testament; very suggestive in terms of our modern world, boiling as it is with change, restless and reaching for utopia. Here is a parable of humanity's helplessness and her willingness to settle for infinitely less than the best. Here is a lesson for the church, for Christians to be the redemptive force in history which Christ intended; not to concede to humanity's transient aspirations under the pressure of her lust for the temporal, her indifference to the eternal.

Here is a man, lame from birth (his

problem was congenital), who was being
carried, laid daily at the gate, totally helpless (he could not even help himself to a
position where others could help him).
"To ask alms"—what pathetic resignation
is implicit in those three words: his highest hope was to be successful at begging!
This is all he expected any longer from
life—alms. Thank God there was infinitely
more prepared for him; an answer which
exceeded his wildest dreams; an answer
he had long ceased to hope for.

There are three lessons of interest in
this narrative. One, a major lesson to
which we will give most of our space, and
two minor lessons, not less important but
minor in the sense that we will devote less
space to them.

He Got What He Needed

The first lesson is this: This man, with
a congenital problem, so completely helpless he could not even help himself to the
place where others could help him, whose
only hope in life was to succeed as a beggar, received an answer quite unexpect-
edly. He *did not* receive what he sought.
He *did* receive what he needed—he got
what he needed, not what he wanted! He
had reconciled himself to a life of crawling

and begging, dragging his useless limbs
in the dust, vegetating. This is not
uncommon in our modern world. There
are millions in America who do not even
entertain the possibility of serious change
in their own lives or that of their posterity.

One of the most pitiful social tragedies
today is human apathy; human nature
reconciled to the status quo interminably.
Human nature reconciled to vegetating;
human nature satisfied with a handout;
millions of Americans, as well as millions
in Europe, Asia, Africa and Latin America
who have no hope burning in their
breasts. This is the inevitable result of a
culture pervaded by secular humanism.
There is nothing to reach for outside of
history. There is no transcendent reality.
Meaning and purpose can be found only
within history—only within the here and
now. The best humanity can hope for is
only what it can do for itself—its own comfort, its own pleasure, its own security.
The physical is the ultimate concern and
preoccupation.

Incidentally, in spite of the popular
criticism of the church today with reference to some of our ponderous sociological problems, it has been the church in
history that has moved humanity off the

dead center of apathy again and again, and triggered the aspirations for freedom, justice and dignity in the human heart. It has not been politicians or industrialists; it has been the church of Jesus Christ. The church of Christ through her missionaries brought education, hospitalization and modern agriculture to Latin America, Asia, and Africa. Of the first 113 universities founded in the United States of America, 110 were established by Christians who dedicated those universities to the propagation of the gospel of Jesus Christ and His Kingdom. The revolution in the world today was triggered by the missionaries of Jesus Christ, putting into human hearts aspirations that would be satisfied with nothing less than God's eternal answers.

But that is just the point: the danger is that humanity will settle for less than the best, material improvement rather than the healing of the nations, a sedative instead of a cure. The temptation is to work with the symptoms rather than the disease; to try to repair and improve the old decaying order rather than submit to God's perfect order. Humanity is inclined to settle for a few paltry coins of progress, when God wants to give us a shining new world of indescribable righteousness and justice and freedom. It is so easy for the church and for Christians to be enticed or cajoled by sentimentalism, or threatened and intimidated by intellectualism to give the coin of social reform rather than the gospel of healing through Jesus Christ our Lord. We capitulate so easily to the pride of men. We are so easily shamed by high-sounding sociological or humanitarian ideologies into offering something less than God's redemptive best to mankind. It is so difficult for us to say, "Silver and gold have I none, but such as I have give I unto thee." But we fail when we give alms only; we fail God, we fail man—even the one to whom we give alms only, and we fail ourselves.

Because humanity's problem is congenital—it is sin in the human heart—there is only one solution: the blood of Jesus Christ, God's Son. This is why Paul could thunder, "I am not ashamed of the gospel of Christ, for it is the power of God unto salvation to everyone that believes; to the Jew first, and also to the Greek" (Rom. 1:16).

Helmut Thielicke, one of the most effective preachers of the gospel in Germany following World War II, who has written some of the most incisive books addressed to postwar Europe and the world, recently published a book entitled, *Encounter with Spurgeon*. Spurgeon, the prince of preachers at the end of the nineteenth century—when preaching had lost its popularity, when modernism, naturalism and humanism had reached the zenith of their influence, when theology had been downgraded to sub-zero, when nobody took sermonizing seriously—was preaching to 6,000 people every Sunday morning in London. And every Monday morning his entire sermon was cabled to New York City and published in American newspapers. In the book, *Encounter with Spurgeon*, Thielicke wrote, "It was not the aim of his [that is, Spurgeon's] preaching to show people that their life would be easier if they accepted the gospel; that it would solve their problems; that civilization would perish without Christianity; that the State and society need religion; that the Christian social ethic is absolutely indispensable; that the world order needs Christian foundations; that all the misery of modern man comes from secularism; that if our world is to endure there must be a renaissance of the Christian west. . . . All this is a kind of high-minded

Christian pragmatism which we are all too prone to promote these days, and which frequently enough is smuggled into the Holy City of Ilium under the guise of a Trojan horse called Worldly Christianity. All this is completely alien to Spurgeon. He is concerned only with salvation. For us and our kind of Christian social ethic, the threatening danger is that we tend merely to explain the Christian ideas concerning the world order, the structuring of society, etc., and then to recommend them for their preservative and productive power. But since it is possible to have the Christian ideas without actually believing, and to be taken up with the social teachings of Christianity, without becoming engaged personally, these ideas lose their connection with the Lord of Christendom and degenerate into ideologies, namely into instrumentalities of power and world mastery. Thus it is possible for Christianity to become merely a pervasive atmosphere, a climate of social order, while faith dwindles away and the matter of salvation is forgotten. Therefore we stand in need of the simple way in which Spurgeon dares to say that what really and ultimately counts is to save sinners. Indeed what really counts is that we get to

Heaven. Anything else is watered-down social gospel, twaddle—including all the talk about the Christian west."[5]

This is the central issue in the church today. Where can you hear the gospel of Jesus Christ that redeems mankind forever? The head of the board of Christian education of one great denomination said recently, "One of our problems is that we have many deliverers of good sermons, and few preachers of the gospel." In the final analysis, preaching of the gospel is what the church uniquely offers the world, and this is that which the world stands ultimately in need of. Let us not sacrifice the gospel for any other message however relevant and practical it may seem to be, for in so doing we are giving the crippled beggar a coin when we might raise him up to his feet to walk and leap and praise God!

Dr. Walter Judd on one occasion said that one of the things that troubled him and many of his colleagues in Congress was the fact that preachers, and church administrators, and Christians in general seem so anxious to get Congress to legislate a kind of righteousness which they are unable to produce in their own congregations. "We can pass laws, but it isn't going to change hearts," said a member of the Senate recently. "We can pass ten million laws, but we'll never change humanity until we find a power that works in the human heart." If ever the world has demonstrated the need for the gospel of Jesus Christ it is this very hour. If ever it was important for Christians to be faithful in propagating the gospel it is this hour!

You Must Have to Give

The last two lessons are so obvious they need only be stated. The first is, you must have to give. "Such as I have, give I thee," Peter said. You cannot give what you do not have. The impotence of many Christians in this exciting, thrilling hour of history is due to the fact that they simply have nothing to offer but a few coins, and alms do not save a sick society. Only can you share salvation when you have it. Do you have it? You can only give what you have and some of us are not giving because we do not have. I implore you to receive the gift of eternal life through Jesus Christ, the forgiveness and cleansing by His precious blood.

You Must Give to Have

The final lesson is equally plain. Not

only must you have to give, you must give
to have. One of the clearest lessons our
Lord taught is that you cannot keep what
you will not give away. He said it many different ways in clear, explicit language. "He
that findeth his life shall lose it; he that
loseth his life for my sake shall find it"
(Matt. 10:39). In the parable of the talents
He said concerning the one who had
received one talent and buried it, "Take
from him who has one talent and give it to
him who has ten talents" because "he that
has not from him shall be taken even that
which he has" (Matt. 25:28,29).

In his first teaching of the Lord's
Prayer, recorded in the Sermon on the
Mount (Matt. 6), Jesus lifted out of that
prayer one petition, "Forgive us our trespasses as we forgive those who trespass
against us" (v. 12). One qualification
Jesus laid down at the end of the prayer is
that "if you do not forgive men their trespasses, neither will your Father forgive
your trespasses" (v. 15). That is plain
English!

Jesus said, "To whom much is given,
much shall surely be required" (Luke
12:48). You cannot give what you do not
have, and you cannot keep what you do
not give! I will never forget one of the

words of Dr. William Evans, great Bible expositor of another generation: "Do you honestly believe that you can get into heaven all alone?" If you have eternal life you had better share it.

Dr. Luke begins his historical record of the apostolic church with these words, "That which Jesus began both to do and teach. . ." He *began* them but He intends that the church, if it be His Church, *continue* what He began in the power of the same Spirit who enabled Him in His ministry. If you had been with Peter and John on your way to pray in the Temple that day, what would you have done? Would you have reached in your pocket, pulled out a few coins and flipped them to the beggar, then walked in pious grandeur to pray in the Temple? Or would you have dared to say, "Silver and gold have I none, but such as I have give I unto you; in the name of Jesus Christ stand up and walk again"? These are thrilling days in which to be alive and know Jesus Christ and His gospel. To have it and share it! If you do not have it, receive it now, and if you have it, in God's name share it.

By faith Abraham, when he was called to go out into a place which he should after receive for an inheritance, obeyed; and he went out, not knowing whither he went.

By faith he sojourned in the land of promise, as in a strange country, dwelling in tabernacles with Isaac and Jacob, the heirs with him of the same promise: for he looked for a city which hath foundations, whose builder and maker is God.

Through faith also Sarah herself received strength to conceive seed, and was delivered of a child when she was past age, because she judged him faithful who had promised. Therefore sprang there even of one, and him as good as dead, so many as the stars of the sky in multitude, and as the sand which is by the sea shore innumerable.

These all died in faith, not having received the promises, but having seen them afar off, and were persuaded of them, and embraced them, and confessed that they were strangers and pilgrims on the earth. For they that say such things declare plainly that they seek a country. And truly, if they had been mindful of that country from whence they came out, they might have had opportunity to have returned. But now they desire a better country, that is, an heavenly: wherefore God is not ashamed to be called their God: for he hath prepared for them a city.

Hebrews 11:8-16

Chapter 9

City of God

In the last quarter of the nineteenth century Marx and Engels gave the world the communist philosophy of history. This philosophy divided history into five periods, three of which have passed; the fourth is the capitalistic period, the "last in which exploitation and class struggle will endure; the period of final revolution, during which all private ownership in the means of production will be destroyed." Then will come the fifth and final period, when "the only economic changes to be reflected in society would be those leading to ever greater production, ever more leisure for all, and history would, with the dialectic, be transformed into universal tranquility and peace." These final periods of history would take place in three phases: first, violent revolt against the established order, followed by, second, a dictatorship of the proletariat, which will, third, eventually usher in paradise, a classless society where everybody owns everything and all benefits of production accrue to everyone impartially.

More than sixty years ago the revolt began and the communist world is now managed by the dictatorship of the proletariat. The revolution, if begun, has a long way to go in many places. Paradise is still as remote as ever where revolt has been successful. And in the Soviet Union, at least, infighting among the proletariat managers has resulted in many modifications; and in some cases, the adoption of certain capitalistic policies and procedures has been found necessary to implement the system. Meanwhile hundreds of thousands totally committed to this eventual paradise have laid down their lives without the slightest participation in the promised goal. Indeed they never had any hope of the promised goal. They simply sacrificed themselves, or were sacrificed, for some far-off paradise that future generations sometime would enjoy. Millions of others have been beguiled and captivated by this promise of paradise and have capitulated to the tyranny of the proletariat dictatorship for the sake of this far-off goal.

Despite this failure of communism in its post-revolutionary stages to approach its revolutionary goal, it accuses Christianity of being an opiate which lures the proletariat to apathy so they will submit to an indifferent, selfish bourgeoisie, with the promise of "pie in the sky by-and-by." And wonder of wonders, there are many so-called intellectuals in our Western world—among them members of the clergy—who have taken this bait—hook, line and sinker; and in so doing they have betrayed their abysmal ignorance of true biblical, Christian eschatology. With what futile hope does communism comfort and cannibalize its pitifully blinded and benumbed disciples, while its leaders piously maintain control of the "people's property," enjoying the maximum benefits of production in the name of the dictatorship of the proletariat? What greater, more effective opiate to the downtrodden masses, to the lambs-for-the-slaughter fellow travelers, than this classless society of universal tranquility and peace to be enjoyed by other generations in the unforeseen future? Talk about "pie in the sky by-and-by"!

But, you say, the comparison is false, for communism has been at work for less than a century, and that promise which constitutes the hope of the church of Jesus Christ was given four thousand years ago to Abraham. And Jesus Christ who came to fulfill that promise—according to Old Testament prophecy, His own words and the apostles' words—died two thousand years ago. Millions have died in the faith of this promise without receiving it; hundreds of thousands have laid down their lives for it. And millions of the faithful have gone to their graves without any participation in the promise. Yes, this is true; and this is precisely the point of the passage in Hebrews 11. The author puts it this way: "These all died in faith not having received the promises." But at this point the analogy ends. For unlike the communist hope which promises fulfillment only to future generations sometime, the Christian hope is retroactive, guaranteeing fulfillment to every one who died in faith from Adam to the consummation of history. In the words of

Hebrews, "These all died in faith, not having received the promises, but having seen them afar off, and were persuaded of them, and embraced them, and confessed that they were strangers and pilgrims on the earth." These "all" who died in faith include Abel, Enoch, and Noah, etc., etc. The grave is not the end of hope for the Christian, but it is for the communist! Those who, thousands of years ago, died in faith embracing the Christian promise are already with Jesus Christ, in glory, enjoying unspeakable bliss while they await the end of the age and the establishment of God's eternal kingdom. God is calling out a people from every nation and language and tribe and color and race and people, generation by generation. He is calling out a people for His name who will live with Him eternally.

I used communism as an example of the futile hope promised by human schemes and systems, but I could have chosen any other of the many sociological-humanitarian-economic-political panaceas proliferated and propagated by the wisdom and ingenuity of man. From the Tower of Babel to the present moment, every effort of man to solve his problems socially, politically, economically, however cleverly conceived and implemented, has ended in futility and failure. They are all 100-percent utopia, which means *no-where*. Talk about pie in the sky by-and-by! All except Christianity fall infinitely short of the glorious, indescribable, universal paradise they promised.

I had the pleasure and privilege of bringing a brief message to one of the homes for the aged here in Washington. I suppose there were thirty elderly women present, most of them in wheelchairs, all of them very, very near the end, very close to the grave. As I waited to speak I looked upon their wrinkled faces, their worn-out, broken bodies and I thought to myself how meaningless are all of the eloquent human schemes for people like this, and there are millions of them in the world. Communism holds no hope for them, but the Bible does! And also for the maimed and crippled, the broken and the diseased, the victims of tragedy and war and unfortunate birth. Paul the apostle declared, "I am persuaded that the sufferings of this present time are not worthy to be compared with the glory which shall be revealed in us" (Rom. 8:18).

Apparently this is precisely what the faithful ones believed and felt whose exploits of faith are set forth in the eleventh chapter of Hebrews. Observe the last verses of the chapter, beginning at 32: "And what shall I more say? for the time would fail me to tell of Gideon, and of Barak, and of Samson, and of Jephthae; of David also, and Samuel, and of the prophets; who through faith subdued kingdoms, wrought righteousness, obtained promises, stopped the mouths of lions, quenched the violence of fire, escaped the edge of the sword, out of weakness were made strong, waxed valiant in fight, turned to flight the armies of the aliens. Women received their dead raised to life again; and others were tortured, not accepting deliverance; that they might obtain a better resurrection; and others had trial of cruel mockings and scourgings, yea, moreover of bonds and imprisonment: they were stoned, they were sawn asunder, were tempted, were slain with the sword; they wandered about in sheepskins and goatskins; being destitute, afflicted, tormented." Then the author adds this interesting parenthesis, "(Of whom the world was not worthy:) they wandered in deserts, and in mountains, and in dens and caves of the earth. And these all, having obtained a good report through faith, received not the promise." Why? Because "God having provided some better thing for us [us now reading this], that they [Adam, Abel, Enoch, Noah, and so on] without us should not be made perfect." Commended by God for their faith, or their faithfulness which is a synonym for faith, they all died without having received the promises for which they had lived and sacrificed. But they were absolutely certain that they personally would enjoy fulfillment one day; that the promise was not just for some future generations.

Abraham, of course, is the prototype of this faith. Paul used him as the supreme example of justification by faith in Romans 4. Hebrews delineates the substance of his faith as follows: "By faith Abraham, when he was called to go out into a place which he should hereafter receive for an inheritance, obeyed; and he went out, not knowing whither he went. By faith he sojourned in the land of promise" (Heb. 11:8,9). Isn't that something? "By faith he sojourned in the land of promise, as in a strange country, dwelling in tabernacles [tents] with Isaac and Jacob, the heirs with him of the same promise: for he looked for a city which hath foundations, whose builder [architect] and maker is God" (vv. 9,10). He obeyed. He went out, not knowing where he was going. He sojourned in the land of promise as a stranger. He lived in tents, not mansions, because "he looked for the city with foundations whose architect and builder is God!" Amazing, isn't it, that this nomad whose home was a tent and whose possessions were largely farm animals and whose life was pastoral in the ultimate, should desire a city?

In our modern world everybody is moving to the city! The city has become the number one problem of the twentieth century. Apparently there is something in the human heart that makes people gravitate to the city. We all tend to be critical of cities today, and some of us are trying to get away from the cities by moving to the suburbs, but we are simply succeeding in creating what is called a *megalopolis*. We are being told that our country will be one continuous city from coast to coast and from north to south along the great arterial highways of the nation. Apparently humanity desires a city, and it shall not be disappointed. A city it shall have. The city of God! Heavenly Jerusalem! Zion! With twelve gates of pearl and streets of gold. Now if that is not to be taken literally, the reality will be infinitely more wonderful! It beggars description, this city foursquare, the city of God!

And it has foundations. How important foundations are. How temporary a superstructure, however cleverly built, however fine the materials, however beautiful the architecture and the style, if it does not have foundations. This city has foundations—which speak of permanence. Think of the buried cities continually being discovered by archeologists, the great urban civilizations which once thrived, then died and were forgotten in history. The city of God will have foundations and will be a permanent city, eternally permanent. Jerusalem is her prototype.

It was at the site of this city that Abraham paid tithes to Melchizedek (see Gen. 14:18) long before it became Jerusalem. It was at the site of this city where Abraham offered his only son Isaac to God (see Gen. 22:9). This was the royal city where the throne of David was established. This is the city where Solomon built the Temple, and Herod rebuilt it. This was the city of the prophets. This was the city where Jesus Christ was crucified and rose again

from the dead. This was the city where the
Holy Spirit of God descended and the New
Testament church was born. Plundered
and destroyed at least four times before
Christ, than razed to the ground in A.D.
70, this city still stands and significantly
remains the site of the most stubborn,
perennial, international dilemma in modern history. Remember Isaiah's prophecy
700 years before Christ? "For unto us a
child is born, unto us a son is given: and
the government shall be upon His shoul-
ders; and His name shall be called Wonderful, Counselor, the Mighty God, the
Everlasting Father, the Prince of Peace. Of
the increase of His government and peace
there shall be no end, upon the throne of
David, and upon his kingdom, to order it
and to establish it with judgment and
with justice from henceforth, even for
ever. The zeal of the Lord of hosts will perform this" (Isa. 9:6,7).

Abraham "looked for a city which has
foundations, whose architect and maker
is God." Did you notice the last line in
Isaiah's prophecy, "The zeal of the Lord
will perform this"? Now the author of
Hebrews is quite explicit that this city
which represents the consummation of
Abraham's hope—the consummation of

the hope of all those from Adam to the last person who will ever live—was to be conceived and built by God. God is the architect; God is the maker. This is not something man has done, is doing, or will do. This is totally and exclusively the doing of God. This is not some utopia which is supposed to evolve out of human progress in history. This is that which God will give! This is that which God will introduce into history, cataclysmically! Catastrophically! This is that toward which Abraham and all other faithful ones through the centuries have been longing and looking, and they shall not be disappointed. This is that for which Jesus Christ died to redeem man. This is that for which He calls and commissions His church; not just to make this world a better, more comfortable place in which to live, but to be busy calling out from every race and people and language and color, a people for His name—a peculiar people, a royal priesthood—to live with Him and reign with Him forever!

You may choose to live and die for the communist paradise if you wish—that classless society for some future generations—and go to your grave without hope. You may choose any of the panaceas of modern man's sociological, humanitarian, political or economic schemes and go to your grave without hope. Or you may look for "the city of God which has foundations." And if you go to your grave before Christ returns, or if Christ comes again before you go to your grave, your hope is absolutely guaranteed. This passage is the sacred record of men and women in history who merited the commendation of God. It is absolutely clear in the record that these faithful ones were indifferent to this life, this world and its order. Indeed they almost held it in contempt. The world was not worthy of them. They were strangers and pilgrims. They "declared plainly that they seek a better country that is heavenly; that they were strangers and pilgrims. Wherefore God is not ashamed to be called their God for He hath prepared for them a city."

This is authentic faith. It looks beyond the grave. It centers its confidence in an eternal promise. It waits and works and suffers and dies with that eternal promise in view. This is that which the church needs today. We are not here just to repair this old world and make it as good as possible. We are here to call men to follow Christ; to call men out of this world into

His church. To call men to look for "the city which has foundations whose builder and maker is God." This is our mission! This is Christian relevance! God grant that we who profess Christ may outlive, outlove, outsuffer, outsacrifice, outdie the disciples of any other scheme or program of men, for the sake of Christ; for the sake of lost, eternally doomed humanity; for the sake of an eternal home—an eternal city.

Postscript

" The great difference between present-day Christianity and that of which we read in these letters [New Testament epistles] is that to us it is primarily a performance, to them it was a real experience. We are apt to reduce the Christian religion to a code, or at best a rule of heart and life. To these men it is quite plainly the invasion of their lives by a new quality of life altogether. They do not hesitate to describe this as Christ 'living in' them. Mere moral reformation will hardly explain the transformation and the exuberant vitality of these men's lives—even if we could prove a motive for such reformation, and certainly the world around offered little encouragement to the early Christian! We are practically driven to accept their own explanation, which is that their little human lives had, through Christ, been linked up with the very life of God.

"There is one other point that should be made before the letters are read. Without going into wearisome historical details, we need to remember that these letters were written, and the lives they indicate were led, against a background of paganism. There were no churches, no Sundays, no books about the Faith. Slavery, sexual immorality, cruelty, callousness to human suffering, and a low standard of public opinion, were universal; traveling and communications were chancy and perilous; most people were illiterate. Many Christians today talk about the 'difficulty of our times' as though we should have to wait for better ones before the Christian religion can take root. It is heartening to remember that this faith took root and flourished amazingly in conditions that would have killed anything less vital in a matter of weeks. These early Christians were on fire with the conviction that they had become, through Christ, literally sons of God; they were pioneers of a new humanity, founders of a new Kingdom. They still speak to us across the centuries. *Perhaps if we believed what they believed, we might achieve what they achieved.*"[6]

Notes
1. Charles Hodge, *A Commentary on the Epistle to the Romans* (Grand Rapids: Wm. B. Eerdmans Publishing Co., 1950).
2. George B. Shaw, *Back to Methuselah*, rev. ed. (New York: Oxford University Press, Inc., 1947), as quoted by Russell Kirk.
3. Oswald Chambers, *My Utmost for His Highest*, the Golden Book of Oswald Chambers (New York: Dodd, Mead and Co., 1935), p. 289.
4. Quoted from a letter to Bob Pierce from Elgin Groseclose, Ph.D., of Groseclose, Williams and Associates Financial and Investment Consultants, Washington, D.C. Used by permission.
5. Helmut Thielicke, *Encounter with Spurgeon* (Grand Rapids: Baker Book House, 1975).
6. J. B. Phillips, *Letters to Young Churches* (New York: Macmillan Company, 1947), intro.